PRAISE FOR

The Pagan Book of Halloween

"This book should help the world to understand the ways of our Pagan ancestors and bring renewed respect for their traditions and beliefs."
—Ellen Evert Hopman, Druidess and author of
People of the Earth: The New Pagans Speak Out

"Gerina's delightful book brings you all the things you wished Halloween could be! As filled with magick as the witches' cauldron of your imagination!"
—Rev. Paul Beyerl, author of
The Master Book of Herbalism

"Well written, enlightening, and lots of fun."
—Raymond Buckland, author of
Buckland's Complete Book of Witchcraft

"Gerina Dunwich has again proven herself to be one of the world's preeminent authorities on Pagan history and lore. This little gem will join her other works as a must have for all serious students of Wicca and Paganism in general."
—George Hiram Derby, Master Practitioner,
Director of Operations, Panpipes Magickal Marketplace

"Gerina Dunwich is at the height of her creative powers. They very best book of its kind available anywhere. A classic of its kind!"
—Lee Prosser, author of
Running from the Hunter and *Desert Woman Visions: 100 Poems*

ALSO BY GERINA DUNWICH

Candlelight Spells
Circle of Shadows (poetry)
Concise Lexicon of the Occult
Everyday Wicca
Magick Potions
Priestess and Pentacle (poetry)
Wicca A to Z
Wicca Book of Days
Wicca Candle Magick
Wicca Craft
Wicca Garden
Wicca Love Spells
Wicca Source Book
Wicca Spellbook
Wiccan's Guide to Prophecy and Divination

PENGUIN
COMPASS

THE PAGAN BOOK OF HALLOWEEN

Gerina Dunwich (whose first name is pronounced with a soft G) is a High Priestess of the Old Religion and an ordained minister of the Universal Life Church, a nondenominational religious organization. Born under the sign of Capricorn, Gerina is also a professional astrologer and Tarot reader. Since 1980 she has edited and published *Golden Isis*, a Pagan literary journal. She is the founder of both The Pagan Poets Society, a distinguished literary circle for writers and publishers of Pagan poetry, and The Wheel of Wisdom School, an educational organization that offers correspondence courses on the eight Sabbats. A major spokesperson for the Wiccan/Pagan community, Gerina has devoted her career and personal life to educating the public about the Old Religion and dispelling the myths, misconceptions, and negative stereotypes connected with Witches and Pagans. She considers herself to be a lifelong student of the metaphysical arts, and is the author of numerous books on spellcasting and Wicca. An occult historian, her varied interests include divination, mythology, herblore, paranormal phenomena, sex-magick, music, and poetry. She currently resides in the San Fernando Valley near Los Angeles, California with her Gemini soulmate and their black cat named Salem. Not surprisingly, Halloween is her favorite night of the year.

Gerina Dunwich

The Pagan Book of Halloween

A COMPLETE GUIDE

TO THE

MAGICK, INCANTATIONS,

RECIPES,

SPELLS, AND LORE

PENGUIN/COMPASS

PENGUIN COMPASS
Published by the Penguin Group
Penguin Putnam Inc., 375 Hudson Street,
New York, New York 10014, U.S.A.
Penguin Books Ltd, 27 Wrights Lane, London W8 5TZ, England
Penguin Books Australia Ltd, Ringwood, Victoria, Australia
Penguin Books Canada Ltd, 10 Alcorn Avenue,
Toronto, Ontario, Canada M4V 3B2
Penguin Books (N.Z.) Ltd, 182–190 Wairau Road,
Auckland 10, New Zealand

Penguin Books Ltd, Registered Offices:
Harmondsworth, Middlesex, England

First Published in Penguin Compass 2000

1   3   5   7   9   10   8   6   4   2

LIBRARY OF CONGRESS CATALOGING IN PUBLICATION DATA
Dunwich, Gerina.
The pagan book of Halloween: a complete guide to the magick, incantations,
recipes, spells, and lore / Gerina Dunwich.
p.   cm.
Includes bibliographical references and index.
ISBN 0 14 01.9616 1
1. Witchcraft.   2. Halloween.   3. Charms.   4. Magic.   I. Title.
BF1566.D867   2000
394.2646—dc21   00–027876

Printed in the United States of America
Set in Minion
Designed by Francesca Belanger

With love I dedicate this book to the Goddess
and Her consort; to Damian; to my mother; and to all
my sisters and brothers whose faith and magick
keep the old ways alive.

Special thanks and bright blessings to
Stephany, Jennifer, Dave and Allan (the Wiccan Twins),
Coven Mandragora, Lee Prosser, and the magickal
energies and mystical spirit of Wilva.

*The Goddess is alive
and magick is afoot!*

PREFACE

On the last day of October, when the darkness of night drapes the sky like a shroud and the crisp air grows sweet with the aroma of fallen Autumn leaves, magick and mystery abound. This is the night when the shadow realm beckons and the veil that separates the world of the living from the world of the dead grows most thin. The great Wheel of the Year has once again completed its cycle, and the time of endings and beginnings has arrived. This is Halloween.

Known by many names—Samhain, Shadowfest, Old Hallowmas, All Hallow's Eve, Festival of the Dead—this special night of the year is the most important of the eight annual Sabbats, holy days that revolve around seasonal transitions and agricultural observances celebrated by Pagans and Witches throughout the world. It is a time when the spirits of deceased loved ones and friends are honored, as well as a time to gaze into the world of things yet to come.

To the average non-Pagan, the most common images associated with Halloween are monstrous and macabre. But to the average Pagan, this jack-o'-lantern lit night is the most sacred night of the year and a time to momentarily put aside one's troubles and enjoy some good, old-fashioned, Pagan mirth and merriment.

If there ever was a "Season of the Witch" it would have to be Halloween. In the Middle Ages, Europeans believed that on Halloween Witches took to the sky on broomsticks to celebrate their Sabbat until the rising of the sun. Hundreds of years later, modern Witches and Pagans still gather every October 31 to celebrate the holiday with rituals, chanting, song and dance, sacred bonfires, traditional Pagan feasts, and various methods of divination—especially those of an amatory nature.

For Pagans the world over, Halloween is, among other things, a night of ancestors, a harvest festival, a time of magick and mirth, and a New Year's Eve celebration. Halloween's roots are undeniably Pagan, yet, Halloween and its celebration should not be restricted to Witches and others who identify themselves as Neo-Pagans. Halloween is a festive holiday that can, and should, be enjoyed by all, regardless of age, cultural background, or religious point of view.

As a new era begins, the Pagan path is shining its light of love on more and more people who are experiencing a growing spiritual need to reconnect with Mother Nature and the ancient ways. Individuals throughout the world are discovering that Wicca (the religion of contemporary Witches) is a positive, Earth-oriented spiritual path, similar in many ways to Native American shamanism. No devils are worshipped and no evil is employed to bring harm to others. Instead, Witches seek to live in harmony with the forces of nature and work positive magick to help, heal, and shape a better world for themselves and their children.

This book, written by a practicing Witch who admits

that Halloween is her favorite holiday, is designed for Pagans and non-Pagans alike. It is filled with history, folklore and myth, magickal spells, authentic Witches' recipes, divinations, a complete ritual for a Sabbat celebration, Halloween superstitions, and much more. It is also the author's hope that it will help put to rest the misconceptions that many people have about Halloween. It is *not* a Black Mass or a night of evil, and its origin, celebration, and symbols have no connection with the Devil of the Christian faith or diabolical rites.

May this book guide you well on your path to magickal mysteries and spiritual enlightenment, and may the gods and the goddesses of old bless you with their light and love. Craft thy magick with love, for love is the law of the Craft.

Blessed be!

SHADOWFEST

Moon of magick,
Blood for fertility,
Druid fires blazing bright.
Spirits roaming,
Wail of the banshee,
Otherworld shadows drape the night.

Raven soaring,
Wings of sorcery,
Eyes like darkest midnight gaze.
Silhouettes gather,
Moment of mystery,
Born again the ancient ways.

—from *Priestess and Pentacle*
by Gerina Dunwich

CONTENTS

The Pagan Book of
Halloween

The Hallowed Beginnings

Halloween has a long and rich history, originating in Pagan Ireland as the festival of Samhain (pronounced sow-in), and becoming All Hallow's Eve in Christian times. A unique holiday, abundant in folklore and fable, as well as in magick and the mystical, it has survived the ages to become the multi-faceted holiday we celebrate today.

More than two thousand years ago, the Celtic people who inhabited France and the British Isles observed a calendar that began and ended with their New Year's Eve festival every October 31/November 1. This festival was called Samhain, a word which means "summer's end," marking the "death" of the old year and the "birth" of the next. It was also regarded as a day of the dead, a night devoted to the practices of magick and divination, a time when fairy folk and gods were especially active, and a festival to celebrate the harvest.

The ancient Celts believed an invisible veil existed that separated the worlds of the living and the dead. At sundown on the last day of the year, this veil grew to its thinnest point, allowing the living and the dead to make contact with each other.

Every Samhain, a deity known as the Lord of the Dead was said to gather together the souls of all men, women, and children who had died during the previous year and been confined in the bodies of animals while waiting to enter the underworld. With their sins expiated, they would be set free to begin their journey to the Celtic otherworld of Tir-na-n'Og, whose open gates awaited them.

In addition, homesick spirits were free to roam the mortal world and return to their old earthly homes to seek the warmth of the hearth fire and the company of their living kin. Families prepared offerings of fruits and vegetables and hilltop bonfires, which illuminated the night sky with an eerie orange glow and served as a guiding light for the souls of the dead. These fires were kept burning throughout the night to frighten away any evil spirits that intended to harm the living.

In Ireland, the priestly caste of the Celts, known as the Druids, are believed to have performed gruesome sacrificial rites on the eve of Samhain. They constructed giant wicker-work cages in the shapes of men and animals, which were used to confine prisoners of battle and condemned criminals. The cages would then be set ablaze by the priests, and their hapless victims burned alive. Sometimes animals—especially horses and oxen—would be sacrificed in addition to the human offerings.

The Samhain sacrificial burning of horses (which were said to be sacred animals to the Celtic god of the sun) was practiced in Britain as late as A.D. 400. After the Pagan temples were consecrated to the worship of the Christians' patriarchal god, oxen were often led down the church aisle to the altar before being sacrificed, continuing the practice of ritual slaughter at the feast of Samhain. Evidence of this exists in a sixth-century letter from Pope Gregory the Great to Abbot Mellitus, which states, "That the sacrifice of oxen in Pagan worship should be allowed to continue, but that this should be done in honor of the saints and sacred relics."

The Druids were said to have held a great mistrust of domestic cats for they believed that some were human beings transformed into animals by evil powers. Each year on Samhain, the white-robed priests would round up as many cats and kittens as they could catch, lock them in wickerwork cages fashioned in the shapes of various animals, and cast them into the bonfires to be roasted alive. The purifying power of the sacred flames of the Samhain bonfires was believed by the Druids to be the only effective way to kill a shapeshifting feline and prevent its evil spirit from rising up from the grave to forever haunt or curse its executioner and his people.

The Druid's sacrificial rites of Samhain possessed a twofold purpose: In addition to appeasing the Lord of the Dead, they offered the priests important omens of the future, both good and bad. These signs were said to have been read in the ways that the victims died, sounds emitted from the fire, shapes of the flames, the color and direction of the smoke, and so forth.

Interpreting the omens for the coming year was an important function of the Druid priests. It was traditionally carried out at Samhain because the psychic climate of the season was ideal, and the widespread fear associated with the approaching long, dark winter and its hardship de-

In Ireland, the priestly caste of the Celts was known as Druids.

manded it. However, in later times the divinatory aspect of Samhain grew to be more personal, particularly for the purpose of predicting future marriage partners. (See the chapter "Divinations and Incantations.")

The inhabitants of pre-Christian Ireland also believed that Samhain was a time when a strange, dark-skinned race of goblin-like creatures with occult powers emerged from their secret hiding places. Resentful of the human race for taking over the land that was once theirs, they delighted in creating as much mischief as possible. Some were merely pranksters, while others were more evil-natured and regarded as dangerous. According to legend, every seven years these creatures would steal human infants or small children and then sacrifice them to their god.

One theory asserts that these creatures were the Stone Age peoples of a wide area of Britain. When the Celts invaded their country from Europe around 500 B.C., they took to the forests and camouflaged themselves with green foliage, which may explain the myth of the "little green men." They frequently raided their enemies' homes under the dark cover of night to supplement their sparse rations and frighten and harass their foes. Many a fearful Celt resorted to leaving offerings such as bowls of cream and oatmeal outside their dwellings at night before going to sleep to keep those of the "conquered race" from becoming spiteful and wreaking vengeance. In Scotland, a libation of milk known as the Leac na Gruagaich ("Milk to the Hairy Ones") was poured on a special stone each Samhain as an offering to the fairy folk. If this ritual was not carried out, the Little People would express their anger by injuring or killing a family's livestock or beloved pet.

Because Samhain was a night on which the fairy mounds (also called the sidhe mounds or faery burghs) stood wide open, all manners of fairies, mostly baneful, were free to walk the earth. Also, any person careless or unfortunate enough to step upon an open mound (at Samhain or any other time during the year) would fall victim to permanent enchantment by a fairy spell and either succumb to madness or waste away from a mysterious and incurable illness. However, according to Celtic folklore, on Samhain night when neither human nor fairy needed any magickal password to enter, an open fairy mound could, like quicksand, pull an unsuspecting mortal into the world of the fairies where he or she would be doomed to remain forever.

There were hundreds, perhaps even thousands, of different types of fairies who inhabited the ancient Celtic lands, but in Ireland (where it was once believed that all cats were actually fairies in disguise) it was the Pooka (or phooka) that was particularly feared on Samhain, when it took great pleasure in tormenting humans. These supernaturals of the night possessed the power to shapeshift, and they were known to often take on the disguise of a black horse with hideous features. It was important for farmers to gather all of their crops before October 31 because whatever remained unreaped in the fields was believed to be either destroyed or contaminated on Samhain night by the Pooka.

The Celts devised numerous charms to protect themselves against the Little People. The ringing of bells (especially church bells) and the hanging of iron horseshoes above doorways were two methods believed to be effective in keeping spiteful fairies at bay. Many people in various parts of the world still believe that iron is a metal that repels and protects against all manners of fairies. It is commonly used in the making of magickal amulets and talismans for protection.

Possessing the power to bewitch or bedevil humans with their illusions known as glamours, fairies gradually found their way into the myth and folklore of many European cultures.

Samhain was more than a night when spirits walked the earth. Like the other great festivals dominating the old Celtic calendar (Imbolc, Beltane, and Lughnasadh), Samhain was also connected with the fertility of the earth and its animals. It was a time when the final harvest was celebrated and when farmers throughout the land brought their livestock down from the pastures and made preparations for the coming winter.

Witches have long regarded Halloween as the Third Festival of Harvest—the first and second being Lughnasadh (August 1) and the Autumn Equinox (approximately September 21). The pumpkins, apples, and hazelnuts that play a part in so many of Halloween's customs reflect this holiday's early link to Pagan harvest rites and fertility magick.

In the first century B.C., Britain and Gaul (as the country of France was called at that time) were invaded by Roman armies and forced to become part of the Roman Empire. The Romans had their own festival for the dead, which was called Feralia. It was originally celebrated on the 21st day of February (the last day of the year, according to the old Roman calendar) and its main purpose was to give rest and peace to the departed. This was accomplished through the recitation of special prayers, the presentation of offerings, and the performing of sacrifices in honor of those who had crossed over into the realm of the spirits.

Eventually, elements from Samhain and Feralia began to merge, but neither the Romans who chose to remain in the British Isles nor the conquered Celts seemed to mind very much, perhaps because the two festivals possessed strong similarities to each other. However, in the fourth century A.D., the Roman Emperor Constantine declared the new religion of Christianity to be the lawful religion, and thus the fate of the Druids and their Samhain festival was sealed.

Throughout the Roman Empire a holy war had been declared upon Paganism and all of the rites and symbols associated with it. The Druid religion was banned and the sacrificial rites of Samhain were outlawed. In the year A.D. 61, Suetonius ordered all of the groves where human sacrifice and augury were said to have been performed to be destroyed, and the Druid priests were systematically murdered in the name of the Christian God. It was believed that a small number of Druids were fortunate enough to escape from the Roman soldiers and went into hiding, never to be seen or heard from again.

The early Christians did not understand the old Celtic beliefs. They erroneously associated the Celtic underworld with the Christian concept of Hell's fiery pit of punishment and damnation, and believed that the Celtic Lord of the Dead was actually the Devil, despite the fact that the two mythos were not related in any way and shared nothing. Because the old Celtic New Year was a day devoted to the dead, the Christians assumed that Samhain was the incorrect pronunciation of the Semitic name Sammael, which means "God of the Underworld."

It was no easy task for the Christians to convince the Celts that their gods and goddesses were evil, their beloved dead were ghouls, the fairy folk were all demons, and the fertility religion they had practiced for many centuries was now the work of the Christians' newly-invented Devil. The Celts were slow to embrace the Christian faith, and many were simply not willing to give up their Pagan holidays and folk practices, which clearly posed a threat to the new religion. Although their priests were gone, they continued to light their sacred hilltop bonfires each Samhain, divine the future, and welcome the returning spirits of the dead.

In more cases than not, as history proves, religious conversion from Paganism to Christianity was accomplished through violent means. In addition to torture and execution, a highly effective method used by the Christian Church to eradicate the rival practice of Paganism was to Christianize it. This was done by giving new names and meanings to the old rites and symbols, including the cross—the very symbol of the Christian faith and the crucifixion of Jesus Christ—which, prior to the fifth century, existed as both a Pagan religious symbol and a magickal tool.

In the seventh century, Pope Boniface IV introduced All Saints' Day to honor God and the early Christians who had died for their religious beliefs. This festival of the Catholic Church was originally observed on May 13, but in the year 900, Gregory III changed the date to November 1 in an effort to supplant the old Samhain festival of the dead. All Saints' Day was also called All Hallows' Day and Hallowmas (Hallow means "holy"), and the evening before it (October 31) was therefore known as All Hallows' Eve. Eventually it evolved into the word Hallowe'en (later spelled Halloween).

In England, All Hallows' was abolished by the Reformation largely due to its Pagan overtones. Communion with the beloved dead and with other spirits was not, in the Church's opinion, a practice suitable for good, God-fearing Christians. However, it was formally restored in the year 1928 on the assumption that the Pagan practices associated with Halloween had long ago ceased.

Halloween was brought to the United States by Irish immigrants in the nineteenth century. Its Pagan roots ruffled the tail feathers of many religious groups at the time. However, Halloween's popularity, especially among the young, outweighed the chagrin of its opposition, and all early attempts to have its celebration banned in the United States proved to be futile.

Today, Halloween continues to rule the 31st of October, casting its spell over young and old alike even though many of its original customs have long been claimed by the cobwebs of the past. It remains the most sacred night of the year for Witches, modern-day Druids, and other Neo-Pagans, and perhaps the most entertaining one for children of all ages and cultural backgrounds.

What began long ago as a Druidic festival may hold different meanings for different people, but one thing that most can agree on is the fact that no other holiday is as magickal and mysterious as Halloween.

Ritual and Revelry

Halloween did not find a place on the American calendar until after the great Irish immigration to the United States, which followed the potato famine of the 1840s. With the arrival of the Irish to the new world came the old Gaelic traditions of carving the jack-o'-lantern, performing love divinations, and guising (which eventually evolved into the trick-or-treat custom as we know it today). They also brought with them their old Halloween folklore. Following are some of the myths, practices, and legends that are inherent in the celebration of Halloween.

TRICK OR TREAT

Every year on Halloween, many children throughout the world dress up in costumes and go door to door in a ritual known as trick or treating. Dressed up as witches, devils, ghosts, and every type of monster imaginable, they collect candy and money and enjoy a night of spooky fun, unaware that their innocent masquerade is actually the remnants of a Druidic religious practice from times most ancient.

The Druids believed that the spirits of the dead returned to the world of the living each year on the eve of November 1. Many of these spirits were mischievous in nature, while some possessed a genuine evil streak and delighted in bringing harm upon vulnerable humans. For protection, the white-robed priests who led the sacred rites of Samhain would wear masks upon their faces to disguise themselves as spirits. This would usually trick the wandering dead into thinking that they were of their number and not flesh and blood mortals. Safely camouflaged, the priests could then gather in the night without becoming the victims of ghosts, fairies, or demonic supernatural beings. The general populace, fearful of being recognized by the spirits of their ancestors, would also disguise themselves, often by wearing clothes belonging to the opposite gender. This confusion would prevent their ancestors from taking them back into the Otherworld at the end of the night. In the mid-fifteenth to early-eighteenth centuries during what is now known as the "Burning Times"—the dark period in history when untold numbers of women, children, and men were routinely executed throughout much of Europe for practicing Witchcraft—masks and dark-colored robes began to be worn by practitioners of the Old Religion when they gathered in forests and fields on Halloween night to celebrate the Sabbat, work powerful magickal spells and healing charms, and perform divinations. Their attire concealed their identities from the spying eyes of those who might turn them over to the local Witch-hunter and scared away any unwelcome Inquisitors whom they might have encountered on their way to the Sabbat.

The wearing of masks and robes that began as a means

of protection for the practitioners and their magick evolved in the seventeenth and eighteenth centuries, into the custom of wearing masks and costumes on Halloween and parading from house to house. This became known as "guising," and is believed to have originated in the country of Scotland. Dressed and painted to look like ghosts, ghouls, and other supernatural creatures, the guisers would parade from house to house, filling the night with song and dance to intimidate malicious spirits and keep all evil at bay.

In Ireland, the soft glow of jack-o'-lanterns lit the way for those who went from door to door demanding tribute for the old Pagan God Muck Olla. Guisers also collected special round loaves known as "soul cakes" and other foods for the dead, and it was widely believed that the charitable act of donating food or money to all beggars who showed

up at the front door on Halloween night ensured one's prosperity or offered protection against a wide range of misfortunes.

By the late eighteenth and early nineteenth centuries, the custom of guising had evolved into nothing more than a whimsical masquerade for children. On Halloween they went door to door begging for apples and nuts and singing traditional Halloween folk songs, such as the following one that was once popular throughout the English county of Shropshire:

> Soul! Soul! A soul-cake!
> I pray, good missis, a soul-cake!
> An apple or pear, a plum or a cherry,
> Any good thing to make us merry.
> One for Peter, two for Paul,
> Three for Him who made us all.
> Up with the kettle, and down with the pan,
> Give us good alms, and we'll be gone.

If the guisers were refused a "treat," they would retaliate with a prank of some sort known as a "trick," hence the term, "trick or treat." Traditional Halloween tricks in England included the blowing of smoke through keyholes, stopping up chimneys with pieces of turf, and smashing glass bottles against walls to simulate the sound of windows breaking.

In the nineteenth century, guising was brought across the Atlantic Ocean to the United States by immigrants, and in the New World it gradually evolved into the Halloween tradition we know today.

THE STRAWBOYS

Long ago, there was a curious custom that took place each year in Ireland on All Hallow's Eve. Young, single men would adorn suits made of white straw and disrupt the homes of those who kept their eligible daughters from the company of bachelors. Known as "strawboys," they would carry out such pranks as unhinging gates, dismantling carts, and stuffing chimneys so that the smoke backed up into the house. Strawboys would often force their way into the kitchens of spinsters, where they would demand a dance (a pantomime of procreation) and steal a bit of food.

In some districts, the strawboys custom was observed on Beltane (May 1), Saint Brigid's Day (February 1, also known as Candlemas Eve or Imbolc), and the Quarter Days: Spring Equinox, Summer Solstice, Autumn Equinox, and Winter Solstice.

THE DAY OF THE DEAD

Halloween, as a Day of the Dead, has been celebrated around the world under many different names and in a variety of ways. In some parts of Ireland, people still call the magickal night of October 31 the *Oidhche Shamhna* (the Vigil of Samhain). In this Emerald Isle there exists an old Halloween saying that states: "All the gods of this world were worshipped on this day, from sunrise to sunset."

Many contemporary Pagans in Ireland carry on the ancient Celtic tradition of "wassailing" apple trees at Halloween. In olden times this was performed to ensure a bountiful harvest in the coming year. Cottage windows are still illuminated by the golden glow of candles burning to welcome the spirits of the dead. "Dumb Suppers" are set out for visitors from the ghostly realms beyond, and plenty of old-fashioned love and marriage divinations are performed by young lads and lasses wishing to know how their love lives will fare in the months and years to come.

Halloween, as it is generally celebrated the world over, is unknown in the countries of Latin America. However, the belief that the spirits of the dead are abroad at this time of year has been prevalent for hundreds of years.

At night, on October 31, it is a tradition for many families to set out food and toys as offerings for the spirits of their dead children who return each year on November 1 to visit. Sometimes firecrackers are lit in front of their houses to ensure that the children will find their way back home.

In some parts of Santa Cruz, a particular custom associated with the Day of the Dead is to scatter yellow marigold petals from the burial site to the front door of the family's house. This serves as a path for the returning spirits to follow. According to folklore, the yellow marigold is a flower associated with the dead. It also possesses magickal qualities that offer protection against spirits that are evil.

In Mexico, the Festival of the Dead begins at midnight on November 1. It is a national holiday of great importance. With skulls and skeletons as its motifs, this holiday honors the dead and is celebrated as a joyous fiesta. Cakes and cookies in the shape of skulls are displayed in nearly every bakery window on this day, and street vendors can be found selling dancing skeleton marionettes, coffin-shaped jack-in-the-boxes containing skeletons, macabre skeleton-shaped jewelry and figurines, among many other gruesome items.

In many of the villages of Mexico it is a custom for males of all ages to go from house to house, carrying lanterns and singing special hymns to the dead. To prevent being attacked or possessed by ghosts, demons, or other supernatural entities, they take care to stay in groups and to steer clear of any dark and deserted roads where the walking dead may be lurking.

Bread of the Dead (known in Mexico as *panes de muertos*) is a traditionally served food on this holiday. Shaped like people or animals, these curious little loaves are decorated with brightly-colored icings or sprinkled with colored sugar, and beloved by both children and adults. According to tradition, each loaf represents a dead soul.

It is a custom for Catholics in Mexico to prepare special suppers for the spirits of their deceased loved ones. The food is set out as *ofrendas* (offerings) and blessed by prayer. After the dead have appreciated the honor and partaken of the food in spirit, the family happily feasts upon what remains.

In some parts of Latin America, it is still customary for graves to be decorated with candles and arches garlanded with marigolds and Bread of the Dead. Families often spend the entire night in the graveyard keeping the candles lit, singing hymns, and providing warmth and companionship to their departed relatives and friends. When the sun rises in the morning, baskets filled with roasted wild duck and various other foods are opened and their contents offered to the souls of the dead, who are believed to have now returned to Heaven. The food is then eaten by the families before they start on their journey home.

Each year on *El Dia de Muerte* (the Day of the Dead) celebrated on November 2, Mexican fairies known as the *Jimaniños* (pronounced heem-awn-neen-yos) are said to come out of hiding and take to the streets, where they dance merrily and delight in playing harmless pranks upon unsuspecting humans. They can also be found roaming through graveyards where they travel in troops.

Jimaniños means "little children" and, according to Mexican folklore, they are actually the souls of children who are not yet aware that Death has taken them from the world of the living. They are said to take on the shape of winged, chubby children, similar in appearance to cherubs. Their legend and lore are known throughout Mexico and Central America, and their origin is believed to be either Spanish or Aztec. They are said to be extremely shy by nature and normally keep their distance from the human race, except on the Day of the Dead, which is their favorite time of the year.

Many Witches of Mexican heritage invoke the *Jimaniños* on the 31st of October when they celebrate their annual Sabbat of Samhain and perform rituals designed to pay homage to their ancestors. Many Wiccans south of the border believe that these playful, seasonal fairies assist their Goddess and Horned God in the turning of the Wheel of the Year.

When the Day of the Dead draws to a close, the *Jimaniños* vanish without a trace, returning once again to the secret places in which they dwell. They are not seen again for another year, according to Mexican folklore.

In France, the Day of the Dead is called the *Jour des Morts,* and like the Latin American festivals of the dead, it is observed on November 2. Churches from near and far are filled with the soft glow of candles, the sweet fragrance of flowers, and the sounds of funeral songs and prayers for the dead. Graveyards filled with wreaths and garlands of immortelles dyed pink, blue, or purple contrast the darkness of death with their vivid masses of color.

In the Italian city of Naples, it is an old All Souls' Day custom for people to pencil their names upon the tombs of their dead loved ones. In modern times, many individuals have also been known to visit graves and leave their calling cards!

In the fourteenth century, many families in southern Italy prepared All Souls' Day feasts for the dead every year, most notably in the city of Salerno where this custom reached elaborate heights. A banquet would be prepared and laid out upon a finely decorated table, and then all family members would leave for church, where they would spend the entire day praying and singing hymns. The unattended house was deliberately left open to enable the spirits to enter and feast upon the offerings of food and drink. (It was believed to be a bad sign if the dead refused to partake of a family's hospitality, for this indicated the dead's disapproval and the possibility that they would work evil against the family.) However, the only hungry souls that feasted were thieves and beggars from the surrounding villages! This custom continued until it was officially banned in the fifteenth century by the Roman Catholic Church, which felt threatened by the holiday's Pagan undertones.

In Sicily, children were once led to believe that the Halloween gifts they received (usually sweets and small toys) were brought to them by the spirits of their ancestors who rose from their graves each year on this day to mingle with their living descendants.

Lithuania was the last country in Europe to embrace the Christian religion. There, Pagans celebrated their New Year feast at Halloween with a sacrifice of domestic animals to appease Zimiennik, the fearful God of the Underworld. "Accept our burnt sacrifice, O Zimiennik," their humble prayer began, "and kindly partake thereof."

If the God accepted the offering on behalf of the entire population of the Underworld, the spirits of the dead would remain benign for another year. However, if they were not appeased, it was believed that they would seek their revenge against the human world in the most demonic manner imaginable.

HALLOWEEN IN THE NEW MILLENNIUM

In North America, Ireland, and Great Britain (with the exception of England), Halloween continues to be celebrated annually. Each year a new generation of trick or treaters carry on the old door to door custom. Pumpkins continue to be carved into jack-o'-lanterns, ghost stories are told in the eerie glow of candlelight, and remnants of divinatory rituals belonging to a bygone era continue to be carried out in the form of Halloween parlor games, such as bobbing for apples. In the various cultures that have embraced Halloween, there seems to be no evidence to indicate that this holiday's popularity has, or ever will, decline.

Masquerade parties are often held at Halloween for children and adults alike. Dressed up in masks and costumes, individuals can, for one night of the year, assume the identity of someone (or something) else, or feel free to reveal who or what they truly are or desire to be without prejudice, embarrassment, or society's disapproval.

Twenty-first-century Witches will continue to observe Halloween as a Sabbat, combining the customs of old with new ones, just as Wicca itself is a blending of ancient ways and modern traditions. Many modern Witches have discovered that the Internet is an excellent source for Halloween rituals, recipes, and occult supplies. Additionally, it serves as a networking tool for magickally-minded folks the world over and for whom Halloween is still very much a "Hallowed Evening." As author Edain McCoy states in *The Sabbats*, "It has always been a time to reaffirm our belief in the oneness of all spirits, and in our firm resolution that physical death is not the final act of existence."

Halloween: A Pagan Perspective

Halloween is a holiday that has fallen victim to numerous misconceptions, and many people today regard it as a night of demonic mischief-making, evil, and unholy terror.

To many children throughout the world, Halloween is a time of the year when monsters become real. The invisible, frightful things that lurk in old cobwebbed attics, dark and empty rooms, creepy cellars, and even underneath the bed seem to become even more terrifying when the shadows of Halloween begin to grow long and the setting sun retreats from the encroaching and ominous darkness.

Halloween fears are not only felt by children, but are common among adults as well. The old saying that "Only the brave—or the very foolish—venture out of doors after sundown on Halloween" remains popular among many country folk in the British Isles. The simple act of walking alone through a graveyard is believed to be particularly dangerous on this night of the year for the blood-thirsty creatures of the undead are supposed to rise up from their cold and silent graves in search of human souls.

Some say that Halloween brings out the evil side of human nature in certain individuals. The number of vandalism acts committed each year on Halloween certainly seems to support this, nearly everyone has heard horror stories about innocent neighborhood children being poisoned by tainted Halloween candy or being injured by razor blades hidden in apples. Luckily such incidents are isolated ones, but it is sad indeed that these images have come to symbolize Halloween today just as much as the jack-o'-lantern.

Halloween itself is not a holiday of evil. It is not rooted in anything of an evil nature. It does not symbolize evil, nor does it advocate evil in any shape or form. Why, then, does it appear to affect some people in a way that can only be classified as evil?

The answer lies somewhere between negative stereotypes created and perpetuated by the media and Christian anti-Pagan propaganda, both of which feed off mankind's basic fear of the unknown.

John Carpenter's classic slasher film, *Halloween,* and its numerous sequels feature a character by the name of Michael Myers—a silent but unstoppable and soulless murderer in a mask who goes on a gruesome killing spree every October 31. The underlying message that this movie and others of the *Halloween*–style genre convey is that Halloween is the appropriate night of the year for evil.

Each year at Halloween, many radio and television shows become a forum for an array of colorful and controversial characters such as teenage vampires, flying saucer abductees, victims of demonic possession, and the like. On the other hand, the annual Halloween media blitz does serve a positive function. It enables many contemporary Witches and Pagans to come out of the proverbial "broom closet," speak publicly about their spiritual beliefs and lifestyles, and address many of the misconceptions that the general public holds about them.

The religion of modern Witches, often called Wicca, does not embrace the Christian concepts of God and Satan, sin, or Hell. With its reverence for nature and the earth, and its roots linked to pre-Christian European goddess worship, Wicca is both a pantheistic and polytheistic religion. Its name is said to derive from an old Anglo-Saxon word, *wicce*, meaning "wise one" and its main tenet is the Wiccan Rede, which states: "An it harm none, do what thou wilt." This loosely translates to: "Live free and bring harm to no one." It is a code of ethics that most Wiccans strictly adhere to.

The beliefs in karma and reincarnation are strongly shared by Wiccans throughout the world, and whatever energies one sends out to others—whether negative or positive—are returned threefold or more to the sender. This prevents the practice of "black magick" from being used against enemies or to manipulate others against their will. Wiccans believe that if you deliberately attempt to bring harm upon others, your efforts will have self-destructive results. In the end, the harm you bring will be to yourself.

Wicca is not a religion that actively seeks converts. Witches who make the rounds on talk shows during Halloween usually do so in the pursuit of bringing education and enlightenment to the masses, and not for the purpose of proselytism.

Modern Witches and others who follow Neo-Pagan paths seek to live in harmony with nature and Mother Earth. Most respect the religious beliefs of others and realize that all positive spiritual paths are but different roads lead-ing to the same light of love. No one religion is right for everyone, and no religion—whether it be Wicca, Buddhism, Judaism, Catholicism—is more valid than any other. Religious diversity is something that needs to not only be tolerated, but celebrated. The good that religion was designed to teach and maintain inevitably turns to harm when one religious group claims superiority over another or tries to deny others of their Constitutional right to believe in and worship the god or goddess of their choice.

The Horned God, who represents the male polarity of nature and is honored in many Wiccan traditions, is an extension of the old Pagan gods of fertility and the hunt. Worshipped throughout Great Britain and Europe for many centuries before the birth of Jesus Christ or the penning of the Bible, horned deities such as the Celtic Cernunnos and the Greek Pan were benevolent by nature and in no way linked to evil in any form or manner. But with the advent of Christianity, the gods of the Old Religion were diabolicalized into the devils and demons of the New Religion in the Church's early efforts to convert the Pagan population to the ways and beliefs of Christianity. As a result, the horns, hoofs, and goatish beards of the old horned gods became the attributes of the Christians' newly-crowned Prince of Darkness.

In some traditions of Wicca, the Horned God is believed to pass into the Land of the Dead at Halloween and remain there until He is once again reborn at the Winter Solstice when the hours of night are the longest. (The myth cycle of the Horned God will be discussed in more detail later.)

Death is one of the prevalent themes of Halloween. However, human or animal sacrifices are not a part of the annual Halloween rituals performed by modern Witches and Pagans, despite the fact that there exists a handful of Halloween traditions that link the Halloween bonfire to ancient sacrificial rites.

For instance, an old Halloween custom in Scotland was for villagers to gather around a bonfire and when the last flame died out, everyone would take to their heels, shouting: "The Devil take the hindmost!" The Welsh version of this custom was practically identical but with a variation on the cry: "The cropped black sow seize the hindmost!" (In a number of ancient religions, including the cults of Astarte, Demeter, Cerridwen, and Freya, the death aspect of the Goddess was symbolized by a corpse-eating sow.)

The connection between Halloween and human sacrifice may have originated in what is known as the Mythological Cycle of Ireland. In the *Lebor Gabala Erann* (*The Book of the Taking of Ireland*), one Irish myth tells of how the oppressed inhabitants of Nemed were required to hand over two-thirds of their milk, corn, and children to the Fomoire (or Fomorii)—a greatly-feared race of evil deities whose name translates to "under-sea dwellers." This sacrifice was said to have taken place each year on the first day of November (Samhain).

The Scottish Halloween tradition known as "burning the Witch" included the burning of a wicked-looking female effigy in a great bonfire called a *samhnagen*. It is said to date back to the time of the Druids, and there is evidence that it was a custom also known to the ancient Babylonians.

Halloween at the Scottish castle of Balmoral included an annual "Witch burning" as late as the reign of Queen Victoria, who was said to have observed it with great delight. The ceremony began by the traditional lighting of a great bonfire, which was attended by clansmen dressed in traditional Highland garb. From a trolley, the effigy of an old haglike Witch known as the *Shandy Dann* would be hurled into the blaze. As it was consumed by the hungry flames, the spectators would cheer loudly, dance, and make merry.

In present-day England, the traditional Halloween burning of a Witch in effigy is not quite as popular as the annual burning of an effigy of the historical character Guy Fawkes, which takes place five days after the celebration of Halloween.

Guy Fawkes, an infamous Roman Catholic who plotted to blow up both King James I and the Houses of Parliament on the fifth day of November 1605, was said to have been executed in a most brutal fashion, along with his accomplices, after their trial for treason. The thwarting of their plan, known as the Gunpowder Plot, has long been celebrated in England by the lighting of bonfires, the symbolic fire-sacrifice of Guy Fawkes in effigy, and fireworks that illuminated the night sky.

Although a national holiday of a political nature, the Guy Fawkes celebration is one that possesses strong Pagan overtones and invokes an undeniable feeling of magick from another time and place.

The Symbols of Halloween

Halloween's sinister reputation may be attributed to its symbols, most of which are of a macabre nature. As Halloween approaches, images of ghosts, goblins, black widow spiders, hideous old hags wearing pointed black hats, and jack-o'-lanterns with gruesome looking faces make their annual appearance, stirring up the subconscious fears of both death and the unknown that inherently dwell within the minds of most human beings.

However, the origin of these symbols, which today are used by advertisers to sell Halloween candy and costumes, date back to pre-Christian times and are connected in one way or another with the Old Religion and its Pagan faithful.

The symbols of Halloween and the history that lies behind each one are important to Witch and Cowan (non-Witch) alike. They not only guide us on our quest to discover the true meaning of Halloween, but, in many cases, they enable us to observe the complex realms of human nature and the mind of man when we see how these symbols and their meanings evolved.

On a magickal level, symbols have played an important

role in the Craft since olden times. They continue to be used by Witches as amulets and talismans, and as magickal tools to increase spellcasting powers, protect against evil, conjure forth spirits and elementals, and represent Deity in all of Her/His many guises. Together, they hold important clues to the ancient history and true meaning of Halloween for Witches around the world.

THE BAT

A popular Halloween symbol, the bat is connected with sorcery and death in various cultures. Its long-time association with the darker side of folklore and superstition no doubt has much to do with its habits of nocturnal flight and roosting in places such as caves and old, ghostly ruins.

Bats were first linked with Witches (another popular Halloween symbol) in the Middle Ages when it was widely believed that all Witches and Warlocks were assisted by demons who assumed the forms of animals. One of the animal shapes commonly used by these demons (or "familiars," as they were often called) was the bat. Bats and their blood were also used in the casting of spells (especially those of black magick), the brewing of potions, and the preparation of flying ointments. When Witches became firmly ensconced within Halloween tradition, all things associated with the practice of the Old Religion, such as the cauldron, the broomstick, and the bat, became connected with Halloween as well.

Today, bats are feared in many parts of the world, and are believed by many to be creatures of evil. They are commonly used by practitioners of the Black Arts, and Voodoo.

Hoodoos (men and women who practice a type of folk magick similar to Voodoo and popular in many rural communities of the southern United States) have also been known to employ bats in many of their love spells, healings, and curses.

The bat is featured in a number of superstitions, many of which are quite ominous. For instance, a bat that flies thrice around a house, crashes into a windowpane, or flies inside of a house is supposed to be an omen of death for one of the occupants. If a bat shows up inside a church during a wedding ceremony, it is an omen of doom for the impending marriage. The behavior of bats has also been used by diviners to forecast the weather, and in some cultures it was once believed that bats were actually Witches in disguise! If a bat was seen flying straight up into the sky and then dropping back to Earth, this was a sign that the witching hour had arrived.

Luckily for the bat, just as it has sinister associations in many parts of the world, there are other places that regard the bat as a good omen. In Poland and China, the bat symbolizes happiness and longevity, and they are greatly respected by the Australian aborigines, who dare not harm or kill a bat in the belief that doing so takes years off of a person's life. In some cultures, the bat is regarded as a bringer of good luck, and is referred to as a "soul-symbol" in Barbara G. Walker's *The Women's Encyclopedia of Myths and Secrets*.

To many modern Witches and Pagans, especially those who follow a shamanistic or Native American-influenced path of spirituality, the bat is a creature that represents protection, good fortune, and rebirth. It is said to be a guardian of the night and a guide to past lives.

To keep bad luck at bay, many practitioners of Hoodoo folk magick prescribe the wearing of a mojo bag containing a bat's bone as a lucky charm.

When painted or engraved upon a bloodstone or heliotrope, the symbol of a bat is said to add great power to a Witch's incantations, and endow all practitioners of the magickal arts with the power to conjure, control, and banish demons.

THE JACK-O'-LANTERN

To most folks, Halloween just wouldn't be the same without the delightfully eerie glow of jack-o'-lanterns, which are often placed on the front porch of a house or on a windowsill as a traditional Halloween decoration. The very sight of a pumpkin with a wicked "face" illuminated by a candle helps to put most of us in the Halloween mood and also serves to welcome the costumed children who go door to door trick or treating.

The carving of a pumpkin is a fun activity for everyone—young and old. However, this custom is far from being a modern one. In fact, it is a well over two thousand years old.

The origin of the jack-o'-lantern can be traced back to Ireland, where hollowed-out turnips, rather than pumpkins, were carved with simple faces and used as hand-held lanterns. They were used not only to help light the way for those traveling the dark roads on Halloween night, but to scare away evil earthbound ghosts—especially those who pursued the spirits of deceased loved ones and prevented them from finding their way to peace in the Land of the Dead.

In Scotland, jack-o'-lanterns were originally fashioned from the thick stem of a cabbage plant. They were called "kail-runt torches" and were used in the same way as their turnip counterparts were used in Ireland.

Their protective powers are reflected in the lines from a traditional Halloween song from Scotland:

"Hallowe'en a nicht o' tine (night of fire),
A can'le (candle) *in a custock* (cabbage stem),
A howkit neep wi' glowerin' een (A turnip lantern with glowing eyes),
To fleg baith (scare both) *witch and warlock."*

Eventually the use of cabbage stems and turnips for lanterns grew unpopular, and the pumpkin became the vegetable of choice and undoubtedly the most prevalent symbol of Halloween for Witches and non-Witches alike.

It is believed that faces, rather than other images or symbols, were originally carved onto the pumpkin because they gave the jack-o'-lantern the look of a head. The Celts of ancient times believed that the head was the most sacred part of the human body, for it housed a person's immortal soul.

Each year on a night that is the Japanese equivalent of Halloween, a glowing paper lantern takes the place of a carved and candle-lit pumpkin. Traditionally hung near garden gates, they welcome home the ancestral spirits and keep all evil-natured, light-fearing demons at bay.

The phrase "jack-o'-lantern" was at one time used as a name for the unexplained phosphorescent light that sometimes appears in swamps and marshlands after sunset. Also known as "will-o'-the-wisp" in the United States, "corpse light" in England, "fox fire" in Ireland, and "witch-fire" in Africa, this natural phenomenon understandably strikes fear in the hearts of many who encounter its eerie luminous glow.

According to European folk legend, the mysterious jack-o'-lantern light is a wandering soul that has been turned away by both Heaven and Hell, and is condemned to spend eternity earthbound and restless. It is dangerous to see one, some say, because they have often been known to beckon humans to follow them into the marshes where they ultimately drown or mysteriously disppear and are never heard from again.

The curious name of the jack-o'-lantern appears to reflect the Church's early efforts to link Halloween and its Pagan customs to Christianity's fearful Prince of Darkness, as Jack is another name for the Devil (especially in England). Yet an old folktale that hails from Ireland attributes the invention of the jack-o'-lantern to a man whose name was Jack.

Disliked by nearly everyone in his village, Jack was notorious for his drunkenness and mean disposition. He was drinking in the local pub when the time came for the Devil to claim his doomed soul. He talked the Devil into having one last drink with him before taking him to Hell, but after they finished their drinks, Jack informed the Devil that he did not have enough money on him to pay for the drinks. He cleverly convinced the Devil to change himself into a sixpence, and then change back to his true form after Jack "paid for the tot of grog." The Devil agreed to the plan. But as soon as he transformed himself into a shiny new sixpence, Jack snatched the coin from the tabletop and, without hesitation, deposited it in his coin purse, which had a silver catch in the shape of a cross. The Devil, rendered powerless by the cross, was trapped inside the coin purse and unable to escape.

Upon his death, Heaven would not permit Jack to enter the Pearly Gates because he was filled with too much greed. He was also denied entry into Hell because he had managed to trick the Devil, which understandably angered his Satanic Majesty to an extent that no mortal had ever angered him before. Jack was eating a turnip when the irate Devil threw him a lighted coal from the fiery pit of Hell. (How the Devil managed to escape from the coin purse and return to his infernal abode is not made clear.) Jack picked up the coal and placed it inside the turnip, creating a lantern which he used to illuminate his way as his restless spirit wandered the earth in search of a final resting place.

Modern Witches often use jack-o'-lanterns as Samhain altar decorations. One is placed at each cardinal point of the magick circle and lit at the start of a Samhain ritual to symbolize each of the four ancient elements: Air, Fire, Water, and Earth. They also serve as a beacon of light to welcome the spirits of all deceased loved ones who return to the world of the living on this night.

Ghosts and skeletons are significant Halloween symbols as they communicate this holiday's ancient link to the cycle of death and rebirth.

Samhain, when spirits of the dead and other supernatural entities were believed to travel freely between their world and ours, was the Celtic feast of the dead, celebrated on November 1. All Souls' Day (November 2) is the Christianized version of Samhain. In many parts of the world, blessings for the dead are performed on Halloween and All Souls' Day. Death symbols are prominently displayed (particularly in Mexico) and are believed to impart good luck among the living who recite prayers and sing hymns for the souls of the deceased.

In the United States, ghosts and skeletons remain popular symbols of the Halloween season and can be found in abundance as costumes and party decorations. However, today the true meaning behind these symbols of death and the spirit world is largely misunderstood, and they are relegated to the same category as vampires, werewolves, and other supernatural creatures whose sole purposes at Halloween are for entertainment and macabre mood-setting.

Many modern Witches display images of ghost and skeletons at Halloween not to instill fear, create morbidity, or raise the dead, but to celebrate the strong belief in reincarnation that nearly all traditions of Wicca and Neo-Paganism retain. In these religions, death is not regarded as a finality. It is believed to be merely a part of the perpetual cycle of birth, death, and rebirth, which is clearly evidenced in all aspects of nature. Therefore, Witches display these

symbols of death to honor this sacred cycle as well as to honor the darker aspects of the Goddess and Horned God who reign supreme at the end of October.

It is customary for many modern Witches to adorn their Sabbat altars at Halloween with images of ghosts and skeletons, especially in the form of candles. When the shadows of this night grow long and dark and the restless spirits of the dead begin to take flight, these waxen representations of death are lit to signify the start of the Sabbat ritual, to welcome the returning spirits of deceased loved ones, and to keep malevolent supernaturals at bay.

THE BLACK CAT

To many people around the globe, black cats are the ultimate representation of the mystery and sorcery that have played a major role in the celebration of Halloween practically since the Celtic order of Druids originated in Gaul (now France) circa the second century B.C.

Black cats are thought to be sinister creatures in the United States, as well as in several other countries, and chance encounters with them are considered to be extremely unlucky omens. The crossing of one's path by a black cat, especially on Halloween night, is an event that strikes terror in the hearts of a vast number of individuals who subscribe to superstitious thought. To counteract the bad luck believed to be brought on by the presence of a black cat, various magickal antidotes have been devised over the centuries. Some of these include spitting on the ground, turning oneself completely around three times, walking backward to retrace one's steps, recitation of special incantations, and, most drastically, the maiming or killing of the cat.

In ancient Egypt, the goddess Bastet (also known as Bast or Pasht) was worshiped in the form of a lean, short-haired black cat, and sometimes as a female human having the head of a cat. Her worship was widespread throughout Egypt and she was one of the most popular and beloved deities belonging to the mythos of that ancient culture. She was a benevolent goddess, and the domestic cat was the animal most sacred to her. So sacred, in fact, that at one time, the very harming of a cat in Egypt carried the price of execution. In mythology, Bastet was a deity who possessed nine incarnations, which may explain the concept of cats having nine lives.

The black cat is also associated with the Greek goddess Hecate (a deity with a strong connection to the practice of

Witchcraft) and to the Norse goddess Freya (who rode in a chariot drawn by cats, and was condemned as a sorceress of the black arts by the early Christians in their conquest of Paganism).

In the Middle Ages, the black cat became a symbol of the Devil and his disciples. Most Europeans at that time also believed the cat to be the animal form most assumed by the Witches' familiar (an imp, or demonic entity, dispatched by the Lord of Hell to serve a Witch as both a companion and an assistant in all of her magickal workings). Throughout the period of history known as the "Burning Times," an untold number of cats—especially black ones—were put to death alongside their Witch mistresses and Warlock masters in the name of God.

The cat has long held a reputation for being an animal possessing both psychic and magickal powers. With its unbreakable link to Witches, Pagan goddesses, divination, and all things of a magickal nature, it seems only logical that the black cat was destined, sooner or later, to become one of the prevalent symbols of the Witches' most favorite holiday.

THE WITCH'S CAULDRON

Often the Halloween Witch is portrayed stirring a large cauldron over a blazing fire. Within her enchanted cooking pot, as black as pitch, mysterious bubbling ingredients are combined to create a powerful brew of magick. Plastic replicas of the Witch's cauldron are sold in shops every October among the Halloween decorations, but these vessels have a far more important function than acting as containers for holding trick-or-treat candy or wassail at Halloween parties.

The cauldron has long been regarded as one of the many symbols of Halloween, and one that has been linked to the Old Religion since the most ancient of times. It is a very powerful symbol, and one that easily invokes a sense of magick just by its very image. It is an important magickal tool that symbolically combines the influences of the ancient elements of Air, Fire, Water, and Earth. Its shape is representative of Mother Nature, and the three legs upon which it stands correspond to the three aspects of the Triple Goddess, the three lunar phases (waxing, full, and waning), and to three as a magickal number. Additionally, the cauldron is a symbol of transformation (both in a physical and spiritual sense), enlightenment, wisdom, the womb of the Mother Goddess, and rebirth.

Since medieval times, cauldrons have been used not only for boiling water and cooking food, but for simmering magickal brews, poisons, and healing potions. They have also been utilized by alchemists and Witches as tools of divination, containers for sacred fires and incense, and holy vessels for offerings to the gods of old. The following are just some of the uses and legends surroundings cauldrons:

If a large cauldron is needed in a ritual, it is generally placed next to the altar, on either side. Small cauldrons, such as ones used for burning incense, can be placed on top of the altar.

❧

In ancient Egypt, the hieroglyphic sign of the threefold Creatress was a design of three cauldrons, and in many temples throughout the land of pharaohs and pyramids, large cauldrons known as *shi* were used for baptisms and rebirth rituals.

❋

In the Middle Ages, it was a popular belief that all Witches possessed a large black cauldron in which poisonous brews and vile hell-broths were routinely concocted. These mixtures were said to have contained ingredients such as bat's blood, serpent's venom, headless toads, the eyes of newts, and a gruesome assortment of animal and human body parts as well as deadly herbs and roots.

❋

In fourteenth-century Ireland, a Witch known as Lady Alice Kyteler was said to have used the enchanted skull of a beheaded thief as her cauldron. She was the first person to be tried for witchcraft in Ireland.

❋

Also in the fourteenth century, a male Witch by the name of William Lord Soulis was convicted in Scotland for a number of sorcery-related offenses. His peculiar form of execution was death by being boiled alive in a huge cauldron.

❋

According to an old legend, if a sorceress dumped the vile contents of her cauldron into the sea, a great tempest would be stirred up.

Ancient Irish folklore is rich with tales of wondrous cauldrons that never run out of food at a feast, while an old Gypsy legend tells of a brave hero who was boiled in a cauldron filled with the milk of man-eating mares.

It is also said that bad luck will befall any Witch who

brews a potion in a cauldron belonging to another. According to a superstitious belief from Victorian-era England, if the lid is accidentally left off the cauldron while a magickal brew is prepared, it portends the arrival of a stranger.

The cauldron and its powers are associated with many goddesses from pre-Christian faiths, including Hecate (the protectress of all Witches), Demeter/Persephone (in the Eleusinian Mysteries), the Greek enchantresses Circe and Medea, Siris (the Babylonian goddess of fate and mother of the stars, whose cauldron was made of lapis lazuli), the Celtic goddess Branwen, and others. But perhaps the most well-known and significant goddess with a connection to the cauldron is the Celtic goddess Cerridwen (a deity associated with the feminine symbols of water and the moon), from whose cauldron bubbled forth the gifts of wisdom and inspiration.

Although the cauldron has traditionally been a symbol of the divine feminine since the earliest of times, there exist a number of male deities from various Pagan pantheons who also have a connection to it. Among them are the Norse god Odin (who acquired his shapeshifting powers by drinking from the Cauldron of Wise Blood), the Hindu sky-god Indra (whose myth is similar to Odin's), Bran the Blessed (the Welsh god of the sacred cauldron), and Cernunnos (the Celtic horned god who was dismembered and boiled in a cauldron to be reborn). Cernunnos is depicted upon the famous Gundestrup Cauldron (circa 100 B.C.) in various scenes with different animals. Believed by many to be of Celtic origin, this large silver cauldron may have once been used in sacrifical rites.

The use of sacrificial cauldrons can be traced to the ancient religious and magickal practices of various European cultures, as well as to some shamanic traditions. Over these cauldrons human and animal victims would be beheaded and then drained of their blood, which would be boiled to produce, it was believed, a mystical substance. Among the Celts, a potion of inspiration was said to have been brewed in such a manner by the Priestess of the lunar goddess.

The cauldron is also linked to the Holy Grail—a chalice that is believed by Christians to have been used by Jesus Christ at the Last Supper. However, prior to its incorporation into Christian myth in the twelfth century, the Grail (as cauldron) belonged to British Paganism as a symbol of reincarnation and the divine womb of the Goddess.

Cerridwen is the shapeshifting Celtic goddess of inspiration, wisdom, and the magickal arts of enhancement, divination, and prophecy. She possesses the three aspects of the Maiden, Mother, and Crone, and is a goddess whose invocation is a significant aspect of both the initiatory and mystery rites of Celtic magick. Additionally, she is often called upon by Witches to assist in the preparation of cauldron brews, potions, and love philtres.

According to ancient Celtic legend, in her cauldron Cerridwen prepared for her son a potion of enlightenment, which consisted of the yellow flowers of the cowslip, fluxwort, hedge-berry, vervain, the berries of the mistletoe (a plant sacred to the Druids), and the foam of the ocean. It was warmed by the breath of nine maidens, and required brewing for a year and a day. A youth named Gwion drank three drops of the potion, which caused the rest of the brew to turn to poison and destroy the cauldron. To hide from the angry goddess, he used his newly-acquired shapeshifting powers to change himself into a grain of wheat. However, Cerridwen transformed herself into a black hen and devoured him.

The use of the cauldron as a powerful magickal tool has not diminished through the ages. In contemporary Witchcraft, it is still regarded as an important part of a Witch's spell.

THE OWL

In the Middle Ages, many Europeans believed that owls, with their glassy stare, eerie call, and hollow whistle, had a connection to Witchcraft. On Halloween night, demons in the form of owls were said to have traveled with Witches and their cats on their broomstick flights to and from the Witches' Sabbat. Many owls, also known as "night hags," were used as familiars by Witches, and some were even believed to be Witches in disguise. Therefore, the sight and sound of an owl was something that was feared by many people.

This dim view of owls was likely to have evolved from the ancient Roman belief that owls were birds of ill omen. Their presence supposedly indicated dire misfortune or evil, and even in our modern day and age, many superstitious people believe that the sound of a screech owl piercing the stillness of the night is an omen of impending disaster or death. (Interestingly, the owl was called a *strix* by the Romans—a word that means "Witch.")

However, not all people related the owl to something evil or frightening. The ancient Greeks considered the owl to be a sacred bird, for it was the constant companion of Athena, the goddess of wisdom and the patron deity of the city of Athens. It was through this association that the owl came to be known as a "wise old bird."

An attribute of the Roman war goddess Minerva, the owl is said to be an extremely lucky symbol for Witches and people born under one of the three astrological Earth signs: Taurus, Virgo, or Capricorn. An owl symbol can be worn in the form of amuletic jewelry, or carried in a pocket, purse, or special drawstring pouch designed for holding good luck charms. For maximum effectiveness owl symbols should be made of gold, silver, or copper.

Many Native American medicine men still consider the owl to be a messenger from the dead, while practitioners of Peruvian folk magick continue to utilize this bird in spells and rituals to combat black magick and to cure various ailments.

BLACK AND ORANGE

The traditional colors of Halloween are black and orange. This is evident in everything from Halloween window decorations to the candles that burn brightly upon the Witch's altar to honor the dead and to celebrate the season.

Halloween is a time dedicated to the dead, and black has been the color most closely associated with death since ancient times. To many people, black also signifies the Devil, evil, and sorcery (hence the term "black magick")—things that unfortunately have come to be associated with Halloween since the advent of Christianity.

Witches and Halloween go hand-in-hand, and the color black has long been linked with the practice of the Witches'

Craft. In the Middle Ages, each Witch was believed to possess a familiar—usually a black cat, a black dog, or a black bird such as a raven or a crow. In works of art, Witches are almost always portrayed in black attire (including a pointed black hat), stirring potions in a black cauldron, or flying off into the black void of night upon enchanted broomsticks.

Black is a color embraced by many contemporary Witches, not for its association with evil, but rather for its magickal ability to counteract evil, as well as to absorb and neutralize negative energy vibrations.

Black is also the sacred color of all Pagan gods and goddesses who rule over, or are associated with, the dark realms of the Underworld. On Halloween night, the energies of these ancient deities are at their peak, and many modern Witches perform traditional Samhain Sabbat rituals to honor and/or invoke such goddesses as Hecate and Persephone.

Halloween's other traditional color—orange—reflects this holiday's ancient connection to agriculture and its celebration as a pre-Christian harvest festival. Orange, the color of pumpkins and autumn leaves, evokes the spirit of the fall season. It is a color sacred to many deities associated with harvest time. It is also the color of the glowing embers and dancing flames of the sacred and magickal Samhain bonfires that once illuminated the night.

Together, the colors of black and orange create a powerful symbol that is rich with legend and lore, magick and mystery . . . the very essence of Halloween. Most modern Witches utilize black and orange candles in their Halloween spells, divinations, and Sabbat rituals. Placed upon an altar or along the boundary of a magick circle, candles of black and orange burn to light the darkness and to welcome the spirits of the dead.

Some spellbooks attribute the use of black candles only to black magick, necromancy, and Satanic rites. However, many magical folks burn black candles for protection, reflection, yang energy, and the wisdom of the Goddess in Her darker aspects. In certain Wiccan traditions, the Horned God and the Crone aspect of the Goddess are represented by a black candle; and in astrological magick, the color black corresponds to the sign of Capricorn. Additionally, black candles are used in Pagan funerary rites and rituals to banish negativity.

Orange candles are used to magickally strengthen health, luck, courage, and the powers of concentration. Corresponding to the astrological sign of Taurus, orange-colored candles are also used by many Witches in spells to solve legal problems or conjure forth psychic visions or messages.

THE SPIDER

In Europe, during the Middle Ages, spiders came to be associated with Witches. Although most Witches, other than the fairy tale variety, have never actually brewed a black widow potion or used spiders in any way in their Halloween Sabbat rituals, spells, or divinations. Nonetheless, the eight-legged creepy-crawler has become a popular symbol of Halloween and the Halloween Witch. It is not uncommon for Halloween decorations to include artificial spider webs with plastic spiders attached to them, spider-shaped candies, and cardboard spider window displays, and so forth.

In some cultures, the female spider's habit of devouring her mate resulted in the spider becoming linked with the Crone aspect of the Witches' Goddess who reigns during the Sabbat. In the myth cycle of the Goddess, the Crone, which is described as the "darker side" of feminine divinity, represents death, the waning and dark phases of the moon, and other symbols of the inevitable destruction that is necessary before regeneration can begin, hence her association with the New Year.

In Greek mythology, Athene (the mother-goddess of Athens) possessed a totemic spider which spun the web of Fate. It was said that from this web the future could be foretold. In one well-known myth, a jealous Athene turned the maiden Arachne into a spider because the young woman's skill in spinning and weaving rivaled that of the goddess's.

Another goddess linked to the spider was Maya, the Virgin Mother of Buddha in Hindu mythology. She was often depicted in works of religious art as a spider or as a woman with the eight legs of a spider, and was said to be the spinner of fate, magick, and earthly appearances.

According to superstition, the spider is a "carrier of evil vibrations," capable of inflicting harm upon both man and beast merely by its proximity. However, to many modern Witches and Pagans the spider is a symbol of good luck and wealth. Those whose religious practices are influenced by shamanistic or Native American spirituality regard the spider as a symbol of creativity and a weaver of the Web of Fate.

Associated with the planet Mercury, spiders have long been used in spells designed to protect against enemies. To discover a small spider spinning its web within a house is believed by many Witches to be a lucky omen. To allow the spider to crawl upon your hands is said to increase your luck.

THE BESOM (OR WITCH'S BROOMSTICK)

The besom, another name for a broomstick, has long been associated with Witches—not so much because Witches were, at one time, believed to fly on enchanted broomsticks to and from their Sabbats, but rather because the broomstick has played an important role in the handfasting and birth ceremonies of Witches and other Pagan folk since ancient times.

In Greek mythology, Hecate, the goddess of the moon, queen of the underworld, and protectress of all Witches, possessed a broomstick that signified sexual union. If a woman desiring children jumped over it three times, she would instantly become impregnated. It is believed that from this myth the old Pagan wedding custom of the bride and groom jumping over a broomstick evolved.

In Europe, during the Middle Ages and Renaissance times, it was widely believed that Witches used broomsticks as their primary means of travel. This was allegedly accomplished through the use of a special "flying ointment" that consisted of various poisonous herbs, chimney soot, grease, and other ingredients. The ointment was then enchanted by magickal incantations and rubbed upon the Witch's nude body as well as on her broomstick. This enabled her to take flight simply by mounting her broomstick and reciting a special chant in the Devil's name. According to folklore, the speed at which a broom-flying Witch could travel was tremendous. Sometimes Witches used spells and potions to turn themselves and their broomsticks invisible in order to escape detection while flying.

Although England once had laws prohibiting the practice of Witchcraft, the use of brooms for flying was never specifically outlawed in that country. During the "Burning Times," many Witches confessed to using flying ointments or sorcerer's grease to give them the power to fly. However, according to Rosemary E. Guiley's *The Encyclopedia of Witches and Witchcraft*, brooms are mentioned only once in the records of the Witchcraft trials that were held in England.

Throughout the Middle Ages, many people in Europe and New England believed in the magickal power of the Witches' flying ointment until early botanists discovered that it was the mind-altering herbs contained in the ointment that, when absorbed through the skin, were responsible for producing vivid hallucinations and the sensation of flying.

To the vast majority of modern Witches and Pagans, the broom is a sacred tool in the practice of the Craft. In ritual, it symbolizes the "sweeping away" of negativity, bad luck, and all manners of evil. It is also used within the circle to symbolically sweep away that which has grown old and is no longer needed, and to enable growth and make room for that which is new. In this respect, the broom serves as an appropriate symbol of Halloween's true and original meaning in its harvest aspect.

Halloween
Legend and Lore

More legend and lore surrounds Halloween than almost any other holiday celebrated in the United States. Throughout the centuries and by its very nature, Halloween has given birth to countless folk beliefs, myths, and superstitious practices, many of which live on as the new millenium dawns.

Passed down from generation to generation, the myriad of legends and lore connected to Halloween is rich with Pagan symbolism. On closer examination, strong links to ancient Goddess-worshipping cults and remnants of magickal beliefs and customs from earlier times become apparent. According to W. Carew Hazlitt's *Faith and Folklore of the British Isles,* "Many other superstitious ceremonies, the remains of Druidism, are observed on this holiday, which will never be eradicated while the name of Saman (Samhain) is permitted to remain."

In modern times, Halloween's legends and lore provide us with amusement; however, they should never be dismissed as merely the inventions of superstitious and unenlightened times. In many cases, they can offer us insights about our spiritual, religious, and magickal roots. They can also help us to better understand the customs, fears, and beliefs of our ancestors, which, in turn, reward us with a greater understanding of ourselves.

FIRE

Fire has always played an important role in the celebration of the ancient Celtic New Year. In Ireland it was customary for all fires throughout the land to be extinguished on Samhain. They were then relit from the central bonfire kindled on the hill of Tlachtga as a token of the new year. Even cooking fires within dwellings were extinguished and then relit in the same fashion. In Scotland, individual family fires called *Samhnagan* were built on the highest ground near the house several days prior to the arrival of the new year. Samhain fires also burned in Wales, where they were called *Coel Coeth*. This old Pagan custom continues to be carried out in some parts of Ireland, the Isle of Man, and Scotland, where the fire is known as the *Hallowe'en bleeze* and is set ablaze in the center of a circular trench, a symbol of the sun, to defiantly ring in the winter season and drive away bad luck and all manner of evil.

HALLOWEEN AS A LUNAR FIRE FESTIVAL

According to Bord's *Dictionary of Earth Mysteries*, Halloween (or Samhain, October 31), Beltane (or May Day, May 1), Lughnasadh (or Lammas, August 1) and Imbolc (or Candlemas, February 2) are regarded as the four lunar fire festivals. In ancient times ceremonial bonfires were brought to blaze during these holidays to ensure fertility and good luck. The Samhain bonfires also symbolized defiance of the approaching winter and its curse of darkness and cold.

Sometimes effigies were cast into the flames to strengthen their magickal effect and/or to symbolize the "cleansing by fire" of any harmful presence or malevolent forces that may have preyed upon the community in the preceding twelve months. It was believed that as the effigy was destroyed by the fire, the object it represented was destroyed also.

The spring and autumn equinoxes and the summer and winter solstices are regarded as the four solar fire festivals. Legend states that they were derived from the movement of the sun. As the Wheel of the Year turns, the lunar and the solar fire festivals serve to interlock the opposite, yet harmonious, energies of the Goddess and the God, and maintain a perpetual balance between the feminine and masculine forces of nature and the universe.

THE ASTROLOGICAL SIGNIFICANCE OF HALLOWEEN

The 31st of October occurs at the time of the year when the sun is positioned in the astrological sign of Scorpio. It is known as a cross-quarter day. This is one of the four points in a year which come between the equinoxes and the solstices, and occur when the sun is in fifteen degrees of a fixed sign: Taurus, Leo, Scorpio, or Aquarius. (Fifteen degrees of Scorpio normally occurs each year on or close to the seventh day of November.)

The date that Halloween is celebrated on also corresponds to the Balsamic Phase of the moon (waning crescent). This phase represents death and the seeds of rebirth, and it casts a mood of darkness and mystery over this time of the year.

Persons who are born on Halloween belong to the eighth sign of the zodiac, symbolized by the Scorpion. According to astrologers, these individuals are generally intelligent, emotionally sensitive, persistent, imaginative, energetic, adaptable, clever with money, and passionate in love and about everything in which they become involved. It is common for Scorpios to be highly intuitive by nature, and many are blessed with strong clairvoyant talents. They make excellent psychics, Tarot readers, and spiritual leaders. If it is not already present early in life, a Scorpio's psychic sensitivity can often be activated by any number of metaphysical methods designed for such a purpose.

The negative traits associated with the sign of Scorpio include: a tendency for intense jealousy, secrecy, shrewd manipulation of others, and vindictiveness. It is not at all uncommon for Scorpios who feel that they have been wronged to seek out revenge in one form or another, and most astrologers agree that people born under this sign make dangerous enemies as well as fierce competitors. A highly suspicious nature is another typical Scorpio trait that can either be a blessing or a curse (if allowed to get out of control).

Many Scorpios, especially those born on Halloween, find themselves drawn to the world of the occult for one reason or another. Perhaps it is the art of manipulating energies by magickal means to gain that which is desired that appeals to them. Not surprisingly, a good number of Scorpios find the practice of ceremonial magick to be the natural path to take.

According to *The Power of Birthdays, Stars, and Numbers*, individuals whose birthdays fall on October 31 are compatible in the areas of love and friendship with those who are born on the following dates: January 7, 12, 15, 16, 23; February 5, 10, 13; March 3, 8, 11, 12, 19, 29; April 1, 6, 9, 27; May 4, 7, 25, 29; June 2, 5, 23, 27; July 3, 11, 21, 25; August 1, 19, 23; September 17, 21; October 15, 19, 29; November 13, 17, 27; December 11, 15, 18, 25.

Persons who are born on the following dates are said to be "soul mates" for those with a Halloween birthday: January 4, 10; February 2, 8; March 6; April 4; May 2.

The following famous people were all born on Halloween: Irish actress Sara Allgood (1893); singer Annabella (1965); actress Barbara Bel Geddes (1922); comedian John Candy (1950); astronaut Michael Collins (1930); actress Dale Evans (1912); actor Eduard "Zorro" Franz (1902); country rocker Kinky Friedman (1944); actress Lee Grant (1927); actress Deidre Hall (1947); NFL tackle Wilbur (Pete) Henry (1897); jazz musician Illinois Jacquet (1922); Republic of China president Chiang Kai-Shek (1887); writer John Keats (1795); actress Sally Kirkland (1944); actor Michael Landon (1937); NBA guard John Lucas (1953); rocker Johnny Marr (1963); U2 drummer Larry Mullen, Jr. (1961); philanthropist Alfred Nobel (1833); broadcast journalist Jane Pauley (1950); folk singer Tom Paxton (1937); broadcast journalist Dan Rather (1931); actress Amanda Sandrelli (1964); lyricist Robert B. Sour (1905); racer Willie Shaw (1902); actor David Ogden Stiers (1942); rap artist Vanilla Ice (1968); painter Jan Vermeer (1632); actress Ethel Waters (1896); and astronaut Terrence W. Wilcutt (1949).

Halloween, a contraction of the words "Hallowed Evening," is a word of Scottish origin and a holiday that has been known throughout the world by many different names. Originally a Pagan festival of the dead, it was called Samhain by the ancient Celts. Samhain (pronounced sow-en, sow-in, and also sahm-hayn) means "end of summer" and is the Irish Gaelic name for the month of November (the official start of the winter season in the old Celtic calendar) as well as for the ancient Celtic New Year's festival. It derives from the name of Samana ("the Leveller"), the Aryan Lord of Death and the deity in charge of ancestral ghosts. Other variations of Samhain include Samh'in (which literally translates to "fire of peace") and Samhuin (pronounced sav-en), which is Scottish Gaelic for "All Hallows." In Ireland, the festival to celebrate the beginning of winter was also known as Samhein, or La Samon, meaning the "Feast of the Sun."

In its attempt to Christianize the old Pagan festivals, the Catholic Church originally dedicated the 31st of October to Saint Michael and called it Michaelmas. They eventually renamed it the Eve of All Saints, or All Hallows Eve.

In England and in some parts of Scotland and Ireland, Halloween is known as Nutcrack Night—a name derived from the old Irish tradition of using nuts to foretell the future on Halloween night. (For more information on this and other methods of divination, see the chapter on "Divinations and Incantations.") Other British names for Halloween include Bob Apple Night, Crab Apple Night, and Duck (or Dookie) Apple Night. In Wales, Halloween is also known as Apple Night and Candle Night. These names clearly reflect Halloween's old connection to the art and practice of love divination.

On the Isle of Man in the early part of the twentieth century, Halloween was known as Thump-the-Door Night because trick or treaters would throw turnips or cabbages at the front doors of those who refused to give them money. Hollantide is another name for Halloween on the Isle of Man, which was the time that once marked the beginning of the church year.

In the United States, the celebration of Halloween as it is known today did not exist until after the Irish immigrants began to arrive in the 1840s, bringing with them their old Halloween customs, such as bobbing for apples and lighting jack-o-lanterns. Halloween was known as both Nutcrack Night and Snap Apple Night in the pioneer days. In the twentieth century it became known in some parts of the country as Trick or Treat Night, Jack-o'-Lantern Night, and Goblin Night.

Other names by which Halloween has, and is still, known by include Calangaeaf, Day of the Dead, Feast of Spirits, Festival of the Dead, Martinmas, November Eve, Old Hallowmas, Samana, Samonios, Santos, Third Harvest or Third Festival of Harvest, Vigil of Saman, and Vigil of Todos.

The majority of modern day Pagans and followers of Wicca prefer to call their Halloween Sabbat by its original Celtic name of Samhain. However, there are certain traditions within the Craft that use the name Shadowfest, or simply refer to October 31 as the Witches' New Year's Eve.

WITCHES' SMOKE

In Europe during the Middle Ages, it was believed that Witches' homes could easily be identified in the following manner: In the morning on the first Monday after Halloween, climb to the top of a hill that overlooks the town and observe the smoke rising from the chimneys of the houses below. The smoke from a Witch's fire will be seen traveling against the wind instead of with it, as does the smoke from "honest fires."

There is no historical documentation found to indicate that Witches' smoke was ever used as evidence in any Witchcraft trials. Instead, a greater likelihood exists that it was merely an old wives' tale, with only the greatest of superstitious minds taking any stock in it whatsoever.

HALLOWEEN FAIRY LORE

It has long been believed that half of all fairies are good, while the other half are mischievous or evil-natured. Additionally, each type rules over a different half of the year. Irish legend holds that the mischievous and evil-natured fairies are most active from Halloween through Beltane (May 1), and the good ones are most active from Beltane through Halloween.

For the best protection against any and all less-than-friendly fairies, an old and simple spell from Ireland calls for a wreath made of dried apples and/or dried heather to be hung over your front door before sundown on Halloween. To increase the wreath's protective power, attach one or more small iron bells to it. This spell guarantees that the fairies will steer clear of your house and all who dwell within it.

To rescue a child or an adult who has been bewitched or stolen by fairies, obtain from a fairy doctor or wise woman a magickal ointment which will give you the power to see the fairy world and its inhabitants. After rubbing this ointment upon your eyelids, go to a crossroads on Halloween and wait for the fairies to pass as they head to their November Eve festival of dancing and merriment. A gust of wind is said to herald their approach. As the fairy troop crosses your path, unaware that they are visible to you, you must quickly sprinkle upon them a handful of dust from the road or a bit of milk. This will instantly render them powerless against you and oblige them without delay to lift their magickal spell from any human being whom they have bewitched and/or return any newborn baby whom they have stolen from its cradle and replaced with a changeling (a half-fairy, half-human child).

In some parts of rural Europe it was believed that malevolent fairies, such as the Gittos (pronounced Ghee-toes) and the Phookas (pronounced Poo-kahs), were responsible for stealing whatever crops were left in the fields after sundown on Halloween. Therefore, it was imperative for the final harvest to be gathered no later than October 30. Sometimes the fairies would strike a day early so they could steal away with the pick of the crop, and sometimes, if they were feeling particularly spiteful, they would curse a farmer's field with blight.

To keep the fairies at bay, many farmers would arrange to have iron bells rung throughout the day on the Eve of Halloween as the final harvest was gathered. According to legend, fairies abhor both iron and the sound of ringing bells, and will stay as far away as possible from both. (This old Pagan custom is reflected in the lines from an old Mother Goose nursery rhyme: "The boughs they do shake and the bells they do ring, So merrily comes our harvest in. . . .")

In Ireland there is said to still exist a race of fairy folk known as the Tuatha de Danann, who become active just before Halloween. If you leave them a small portion of your harvest as an offering on October 31, these trooping fairies (who are said to have created Ireland's ancient stone megaliths) will reward you by blessing your home. Fairy blessings are very magickal and extremely powerful, and a home that receives their blessings is sure to remain free of misfortune and unhappiness for an entire year.

In certain traditions of Wicca, it is customary for fairies to be invited to observe or participate in certain rituals. Traditionally, the most ideal time of the year to make contact with the fairy race is from Halloween through Candlemas (also called Imbolc, celebrated on February 2).

A favorite is Robin Goodfellow, a panpipe-playing English fairy who is also known by the names Puck, Jack Robinson, and Lord of the Greenwood, is said to possess the head of a young male and the hirsute body of a goat. Playful and lusty by nature, he is identified with the Horned God in many Pagan circles. Each year, he becomes active at the time of the spring equinox (when the Horned God in his myth cycle is youthful) and disappears from sight on Halloween (the time of the year when the Horned God dies).

The following types of fairy folk are said to be associated, in one way or another, with Halloween: the Beansidhe (pronounced ban-shee, a female spirit whose lamentations are believed to herald a death in the family, according to old Irish folklore); the Erlkonig (the German male equivalent of the Beansidhe, whose name means "Elf King"); the Fylgiar (a type of fairy that, according to Icelandic folklore, makes its appearance to humans who are soon to die); Gittoes; Goblins/Hobgoblins (evil fairies, skilled in the art of shapeshifting and said to be once populous in England); Phookas (a race of nocturnal Irish hobgoblins said to be ill-tempered and extremely ugly); and the Tuatha de Danann.

THE CRONE GODDESS OF SAMHAIN

Nicnevin, a Pagan goddess who hails from the old religion of pre-Christian Scotland, is known as the Crone Goddess of Samhain. She is said to be a deity of great wisdom and magickal aptitude, and many modern Witches (especially those of Scottish heritage and/or those who follow a Scottish tradition of Wicca) invoke her presence during Halloween rituals for empowerment and protection against all forms of negativity. Witchcraft and the magickal arts are the realms that this goddess governs, and she represents the imminent onset of the dark half of the year.

THE BLUE-FACED HAG

In Celtic/Scottish mythology, Cailleach Bheur is the white-haired goddess of winter, depicted as a lean, blue-faced hag. Each year on the 31st of October she is reborn. She is the bringer of snow, and was also known as a "spirit of disease" who brought death in winter.

Like the Hindu goddess Kali, Cailleach was both a destroyer and a creator. She founded many races of people and had numerous consorts, whom she outlived. According to one myth, she created the world, and the stones that dropped from her apron formed the Earth's mountain ranges.

Her name is thought to mean either "old woman" or "veiled one," and it is said that the ancient name for Scotland—Caledonia—meant "the land given by Cale, or the Cailleach." In her honor, the ancient Celts erected sacred standing stones, and up until recent times, many superstitious farmers throughout Scotland feared that cutting the last remaining stalk of grain would bring down her wrath.

According to ancient legend, Cailleach reigns each year from the eve of Samhain until the eve of Beltane (April 30), at which time the goddess Brigit deposes her and she becomes transformed into stone. Many scholars believe that the mythical blue-faced, cave-dwelling cannibal goddess known as Black Annis is a derivative of Cailleach Bheur of the Highlands.

THE DAGDA AND THE MORRIGAN

In Irish mythology, Samhain was a time when Dagda (the male tribal god known as "the Good God") and Morrigan (a goddess of both fertility and destruction, who is frequently referred to as "the Queen of Demons" or "the Phantom Queen" in Irish texts) come together as lovers. Their mating ritual was said to have taken place as Morrigan bestrode the River Unius. The Celts strongly believed that through the sexual union of these two deities, the continuing prosperity of the tribe, the success of all of their undertakings, and the fertility of their crops and livestock were assured in the coming year.

In some versions of the myth, the goddess—in her aspect of the aged Crone—is magickally rejuvenated each Samhain by the act of sexual intercourse with her consort, and transforms one again into a woman of youth and beauty. In this goddess aspect she is known as the Virgin.

AN OLD SEAFARING LEGEND

Sailors and fishermen the world over have long associated the waves of the ocean with a variety of unusual beliefs. One old seafaring legend claims that the souls of all men who have drowned at sea rise up from the depths of the oceans each Halloween (as well as Easter and Christmas) to ride the "white horses" that form on top of the waves.

HALLOWEEN PUMPKIN LORE

According to an old occult tradition, pumpkins that are to be carved into Halloween jack-o'-lanterns should always be planted on Good Friday. This supposedly endows them with the magickal power to keep at bay all evil supernaturals that haunt the world of the living after the sun sets on Halloween night.

Additionally, the rules of lunar gardening (which are observed by many modern Witches and Pagans) call for pumpkins to be planted in the ground when the moon is waxing and positioned in one of the "fruitful" signs of the zodiac: Cancer, Scorpio, Pisces, Taurus, Capricorn, or Libra.

You should also take care not to point at any pumpkins as they grow in their patches because this will cause them to rot, and always use a knife with a white handle when harvesting pumpkins and carving them into jack-o'-lanterns. Using a knife with a black handle is thought by many superstitious souls to be unlucky.

PRAYERS TO THE SUN

In ancient times, many Pagan folks in various parts of the world observed Halloween by offering prayers and thanks to their solar deity for the harvest, which, at this time of the year, was safely stored against the darkness and bitter cold of the coming winter.

Many modern Witches and Pagans carry on this

centuries-old Halloween custom by including a thanks-giving prayer to the god of the sun in their Sabbat rite.

PITCHFORKS AND MAGICK MOUNTAINS

There is an old peasant custom associated with Halloween that still exists in some parts of Scotland and Ireland. Beneath the enchanting Halloween moon straw-laden pitchforks are set ablaze and then waved aloft. It is said that this singes the besoms (broomsticks) of any airborne Witches who may be hovering near by.

A similar Halloween custom can be found in Scandinavia, where it was once believed that burning straw possessed the power to drive all evil-natured Witches back to the magick mountain known as the Blocksberg. Scandinavian folklore holds that this is where the powerful and fearful Queen of the Witches dwelled. It is also said to be the place where Witches from near and far gathered each year to celebrate their Great Sabbat. (In a similar legend hailing from Germany in the Middle Ages, a magick mountain called the Brocken served as the Witches' covenstead.)

In an Irish legend dating back to ancient times, a magickal hill called Tara served as the ancestral seat of the gods. Each year at Samhain, a harp-playing goblin called Aillen would cast a sleep enchantment over all with his magickal music and then set fire to the King's great palace on the hill (which had "seven views on every side"), destroying Tara. The goblin's evil magick was finally overcome by a brave hero named Finn, who prevented himself from falling under the goblin's spell of slumber by inflicting pain upon his own forehead with the sharp point of his spear.

Centuries ago in parts of Great Britain and the United States, it was believed that if a deceased person's soul was not released from its sins before the corpse was laid to rest in the Earth, it would not pass into the glory of paradise, but would instead be doomed to roam the Earth each Halloween as one of the walking dead.

To remedy this, a man or woman known as a "sin-eater" would be employed to ritually absorb the sins of the deceased by consuming food and drink placed upon the dead person's body. After the sin-eater's duties had been performed to the satisfaction of the bereaved family, he or she would be paid (usually sixpence) and then quickly sent away. According to folklore, the only way the sin-eater can, in turn, expel the sins is through another sin-eater.

Sin-eating was a common funeral custom in the English county of Hereford, and those employed for this unusual function usually hailed from poor families where the role of sin-eating was passed down from one generation to the next. In certain rural communities, sin-eating is a practice that continues to be performed at wakes in modern times.

THE SWAN-WOMAN

In an old Celtic myth, an enchantment placed on a beautiful maiden named Caer caused her to change into a swan every other year at the festival of Samhain. Only the love of a god could break the magickal spell.

Oenghus mac Oc (Oenghus, "the Young Son") was a god who presided over love and youth. He was also the helper of many star-crossed lovers. After Caer's beautiful face appeared to him in a dream, he became quite smitten with her, falling into what can only be described as a deep lovesickness. He learned that she, in bird-form, lived among a troop of 150 female swan companions. If he could distinguish her from the others, she would be free to leave with him if she chose to do so. However, the only way he could gain entry into Caer's world to rescue her from the spell was to join her in transformation.

After using his divine powers to change himself into a swan at Samhain, Oenghus searched for his bewitched love at a lake where each pair of swans was linked by a chain of silver. However, because Caer was special, a golden chain decorated her neck, and this is how Oenghus was able to correctly identify her. He called to her and they circled the lake three times.

The romantic tale of Caer and Oenghus concludes with the two swan lovers' escape to Oenghus's *sidh* (fairy mound) at Brugh na Boinne after their song-filled flight cast an enchantment of sleep over all who heard it. This magickally-induced slumber lasted for three days and nights.

LEGEND AND LORE FROM BRITTANY

In the not too distant past, it was a rather common custom in Brittany (France) for bellmen and "death singers" to make their rounds prior to the midnight hour on Halloween, warning all near and far that the spirits of the dead were approaching.

In each home, special candles were lit, prayers were recited to bless the good spirits, as well as to protect against the evil ones, and a food spread known as a "mute supper" (traditionally consisting of bread, salt, apples, and cider) was set out as an offering for departed friends and relatives.

In Brittany during the Middle Ages, protection against evil spirits who roamed the Earth on Halloween was sought through special stone lighthouses known as "Lanterns of the Dead." They would be lit shortly before nightfall, and it was believed that their glowing lights kept all dark-natured supernatural entities at bay.

WASSAILING AT SEA

In parts of Scotland during the Middle Ages, a wassailing custom was performed on October 31 to ensure a plentiful supply of fish and fertility in the coming year.

M. Martin's *Western Islands of Scotland* (1703) states that "The Inhabitants . . . had an ancient Custom to sacrifice to a Sea God . . . at Hallow-tide." One person among the islanders would be chosen to wade into the sea with a chalice of ale in his hand. In a loud voice he would cry: "I give you this cup of ale, hoping that you'll be so kind as to send up plenty of sea-ware, for enriching our ground." The ale would then be poured into the sea as an offering to the ancient Pagan deity that was believed to inhabit its mysterious depths.

This custom, which was thought to be a "powerful means to procure a plentiful crop," was banned by the Catholic Church around 1670 for being what Christians regarded as a relic of the heathen sacrificial rites of the Druidic priesthood.

The custom of wassailing is one that dates back to antiquity, but is in no way limited strictly to Halloween. In many parts of the world, wassailing is a tradition strongly connected to Christmas, New Year celebrations, and the Twelfth Night (the evening of, or before, Twelfth Day—the twelfth day after Christmas, when special festivities were held).

THE CHURCHYARD WALKER

In Somerset, England, it was once believed that if a person lingered by the church gate at the midnight hour on Halloween to watch for the apparitions of the men and women who were destined to die within the coming year, he or she ran the risk of becoming the "churchyard walker" (a ghostly guardian of the graveyard) and remaining in that form until some other person was foolish enough to disturb the dead on All Hallows' Eve.

TAM LIN

Folklore holds that the thresholds of Halloween and May Day (Beltane) are prominent times for both mortals and supernaturals to shapeshift. This can be seen in the old British border ballad of Tam Lin—a young man captured by the Queen of Fairies after falling from his horse on Halloween while out riding in the woods with his grandfather. He is magickally transformed into an "elfin knight" and doomed to haunt the forest for seven years and then be offered up on Halloween as the fairies' seven-year tribute to the Prince of Darkness.

Tam Lin's lover, a fair young maiden named Janet (sometimes called Jenny), ventures to the well in the wood and conjures her lover by picking a rose. He appears and informs her of the only way to disenchant him, which must be carried out at the witching hour on Halloween. Carefully following his instructions, Janet goes to a place called Miles Cross and waits for the elfin knight to come on his "milk-white steed" in the Fairy Rade (a fairy procession). She hears "the bridles ring" and lets the riders of the black and the brown horses pass by. Spotting her lover upon his white horse, she quickly runs to him and pulls him down. She holds him fast as he changes through countless monstrous shapes, including an adder snake, a growling bear, a ferocious lion, and a burning red-hot ember.

Much to the dismay of the angered Queen of Fairies, Janet is successful in maintaining her hold until the crowing of the cock the next morning breaks the wicked fairy spell that held Tam Lin a helpless prisoner.

No longer under the Fairy Queen's enchantment, Tam Lin returns once again to human form, blythe as "a bird in spring." He and Janet eventually wed and live happily ever after.

HALLOWEEN APPLE LORE

If you bury an apple in your garden beneath the rays of the moon on Halloween night, it will nourish the souls of the dead who roam the Earth at this time of the year.

Legend also has it that an apple buried in the ground on the last day of October will attract unicorns. These magickal horselike creatures are said to live beneath apple trees and can sometimes be spotted frolicking in apple orchards on quiet, mist-filled mornings.

In days gone by, it was believed by some apple growers that a fine crop of apples could be guaranteed in the coming year simply by burying thirteen leaves from a harvested apple tree on Halloween. However, to be effective, this ritual was required to be carried out secretly and in complete silence. To utter even one word at any time during its performance was said to cause the power of the apple spell to be broken.

If you eat an apple on Halloween night before going to bed, it is said that you will not suffer any illnesses within the next twelve months. (Eating a slice from three apples on Halloween also ensures a year filled with good luck, according to superstition.) Folk healers have long connected the apple with the maintenance of good health, hence the old expression: "An apple a day keeps the doctor away."

On Halloween in the year 1970, the Parks Department of New York City granted the Witches International Craft Associates (W.I.C.A.) a permit to hold a "Witch-In." The festive event was held in Sheep Meadow in Central Park and attended by well over one thousand persons. It was one of the first public Pagan gatherings to be held in the United States, paving the way for such events as Circle Sanctuary's Spirit Gathering, the CraftWise Pagan Gatherings, Starwood, Witchstock, and others.

The New Reformed Orthodox Order of the Golden Dawn was formed on Halloween in the year 1967. The 31st of October is also the charter date for the Covenant of the Goddess—the largest federation of covens and solitary elders from different Wiccan traditions.

Halloween Herb Lore

Herbs have long had a strong connection to Halloween, contributing to the magick, divination, and Pagan lore that surround this special night of the year. In our contemporary era, a good number of herbs have managed to retain their link to Halloween, as the art and practice of using herbs for magical purposes, or wortcunning, remains an essential part of the Witch's Craft. Empowered by the energies of Mother Earth and her elementals, herbs are truly blessed with magick, and each has its own story to tell.

SABBAT HERBS, OILS, AND TEAS

According to Edain McCoy's *The Sabbats*, the following plants correspond to the Sabbat of Samhain: allspice, apples (to honor the dead), catnip, gourds (used in past times for protection against evil spirits), mugwort (an herb long associated with psychic workings and the divinatory arts), and sage (to celebrate reincarnation, as well as to symbolize the wisdom of the Crone).

The following ritual oils are said to correspond to

Samhain: basil (also known as witches' herb, and ruled by the planet Mars and the element of Fire), camphor (ruled by the Moon and the element of Water), clove (ruled by Jupiter and the element of Fire), frankincense (ruled by the Sun and the element of Fire), lilac (ruled by Venus and the element of Water), yarrow (ruled by Venus and the element of Water), and ylang-ylang (planetary and elemental ruler unknown).

The attunement teas that correspond to Samhain are (individually or blended): angelica, apple, catnip, Indian hyppo, sage, and valerian. Witches often drink these teas prior to performing a Sabbat ritual to aid meditation and to bring themselves into spiritual harmony.

ROWAN TREE

In the Scottish town of Strathspey, an eighteenth-century Halloween custom was to make a hoop of rowan tree branches, through which all the sheep and lambs would be made to pass. This would be carried out throughout the day and night on Samhain in the belief that the tree's protective powers preserved the animals from the evil effects of elves and wicked Witches.

Rowan, a type of mountain ash reputed to repel sorcerers, evil spirits, and fairy folk, has long been used as a protective charm for animals. In the book, *Daemonologie*, it is written that branches of rowan were once knitted to the hair or tails of cattle to keep them safe from the evil eye.

Ruled by the planet Saturn and under the elemental influence of Water, hemp has long been used in spells and divinations of an amatory nature. In England, it was once believed that when hemp seed was tossed over the shoulder at midnight on Halloween, a vision of one's future husband or wife would appear.

In the Victorian era, many Witches burned a combination of hemp and mugwort as a scrying incense to facilitate the awakening of their psychic senses. This practice was often performed on Halloween night prior to, as well as during, the traditional scrying of crystal balls and magick mirrors to gain visions.

In the 1930s, laws were enacted in the United States to restrict the use and sale of hemp, which greatly resulted in the decline of the plant's magickal use among Witches and diviners. However, as the twenty-first century dawns, many pro-hemp activist groups and individuals are seeking to repeal the existing laws that make hemp illegal in this country.

"FLYING OINTMENT" HERBS

In Europe during the height of the Witch-burning era, it was believed that Witches (especially those of the female gender) used a special grease-based concoction known as a "flying ointment," which enabled them to fly, with or without broomsticks, to and from their Halloween Sabbat.

Various flying ointment recipes have been handed down from generation to generation, and a number of these have appeared in magickal textbooks known as grimoires. They typically call for ingredients such as the fat of a newborn infant, chimney soot, and the blood of a bat. In addition, herbs of a poisonous and/or hallucinogenic nature are required.

The most common herbs used in flying ointments were:

Aconite Ruled by the planet Saturn and the element of Water, sacred to the goddess Hecate. Also known as monkshood and wolf's bane.

Belladonna Ruled by the planet Saturn and the element of Water. Known by numerous folk names, including banewort, deadly nightshade, devil's weed, sorcerer's berry, and witch's berry.

Cinquefoil Ruled by the planet Jupiter and the element of Fire.

Foxglove Ruled by the planet Venus and the element of Water. Also known as fairy weed, witches' bells, and witches' thimbles.

Hellebore root Ruled by the planet Saturn and the element of Water.

Hemlock Ruled by the planet Saturn and the element of Water. Sacred to the goddess Hecate. Also known as warlock weed.

Hemp Ruled by the planet Saturn and the element of Water, and known by numerous folk names.

Henbane Ruled by the planet Saturn and the element of Water. Also known as black nightshade and devil's eye.

Mandrake Ruled by the planet Mercury and the element of Fire. Sacred to the goddess Hecate. Known by numerous folk names, including Circe's plant or herb of Circe, hexenmannchen (German for witch's mannikin), mandragora, and sorcerer's root.

Poplar leaves Ruled by the planet Saturn and the element of Water.

Poppy juice Ruled by the Moon and the element of Water. Sacred to the ancient Greek god Hypnos.

HAZEL

The hazel, a nut-bearing bush or small tree ruled by the Sun and the element of Air, is a very magickal gift from Mother Nature. It was regarded as sacred by the ancient Celts, for whom it represented wisdom, occult knowledge, and divination. They believed the hazel to be a "magic tree that wizards love."

The hazelnut, more than any other type of nut, has long been associated with the Halloween tradition of divination, particularly the amatory type. Many Witches traditionally eat a hazelnut on Halloween prior to scrying crystal balls or other divining methods to see into the future in the belief that it will help to strengthen and/or facilitate their powers of clairvoyance. Hazelnuts are also carried in charm bags on Halloween to ensure fertility throughout the coming year. Nine hazelnuts, strung together to make an amulet and then hung in the house on Halloween, are said to attract good luck and offer protection against all forms of evil and negativity. (An excellent Halloween hazelnut spell can be found in Pauline Campanelli's *Wheel of the Year: Living the Magical Life.*)

The Druids were known to employ wands of hazel in

their sacred rites. However, the celebrated power of the hazel was not linked only to the Pagan sects. The Celtic Christian bishops also possessed staffs that were carved from hazel. So great is the occult and psychic energies generated by the hazel tree that its wood has long been used by Witches in the making of magickal wands, and its forked branches continue to be used the world over as divining rods to locate underground water or minerals.

On the Isle of Skye, it was once traditional for hazelnuts to be gathered on the day before Halloween. In a hazel grove adjacent to an aged wishing well, children would gather from near and far and fill their baskets to the brim with nuts.

According to an old Celtic myth, a hazel tree overhanging the Well of Enchantment grew the Nuts of Knowledge, which were potent with magickal power. Every Halloween, the nuts ripened, turning a deep scarlet-red, and fell from the tree into the hungry mouth of the Salmon of Knowledge.

HEATHER

Ruled by the planet Venus and under the elemental influence of Water, heather has long been used by practitioners of the magickal arts who wish to conjure up ghosts—both good and bad. Many Witches burn dried heather at Halloween to invite the spirits of their deceased loved ones to visit.

Folklore holds that sprigs of white heather attract good luck and ensure happiness. This may explain why many brides choose white heather for their headpieces and why a number of politicians wear it in their buttonholes when campaigning.

However, take care not to bring any other type of heather into your house—on Halloween or at any other time of the year—for this is said to be a sign of death, according to an old Welsh belief.

Superstitions and Omens

Halloween possesses its fair share of omens—some good and some not so good. Such is the way with omens. Unfortunately, there is no way of knowing the actual means by which most of Halloween's omens came to be born. Their illusive origins add to the mystery of the ancient mind and its workings.

The art and practice of reading omens began long ago, perhaps as far back as prehistoric times. It is quite conceivable that our cave-dwelling ancestors, fearing phenomena that they did not understand, regarded such natural events as lightning, earthquakes, and solar eclipses as important omens—maybe even warning signs that their gods were displeased in some way.

Since the dawn of early man, countless methods of interpreting the future and the unknown by omens have been devised. Omen reading, which satisfies to some extent the natural human desire to gain insight to one's destiny, is an "occult science" that has been, and continues to be, practiced the world over.

According to *The Shepherd's Prognostication* (first published in the year 1729), "All-hallows-tide" (Halloween) is the traditional time to read weather omens. To discover if the coming winter will be cold or warm, cut a chip from a beech tree on October 31 and examine it to see if it is wet or dry. If wet, this is a sign that the winter will be bitter cold. If dry, expect a warmer than normal winter season.

CANDLE SUPERSTITIONS

Many people in various parts of the world consider it to be extremely unlucky to look at their reflection in a mirror by candlelight on Halloween night. It was believed that gazing into a mirror illuminated by the light of a candle (especially a red or black one) would cause the Devil to appear in the reflection.

A burning candle placed inside a hollowed-out pumpkin or jack-o'-lantern on Halloween works to keep evil spirits and demons at bay.

For good luck, burn black and orange candles on Halloween. (Black and orange are the traditional colors of Halloween, and on this day their magickal vibrations are at their peak.)

Practitioners of the black art of sorcery believe that the act of inscribing an enemy's name upon a skull-shaped candle and then burning it at the witching hour on Halloween will bring harm or death to that foe.

If a candle should suddenly go out by itself on Halloween as though being blown out by wind or by breath,

this is said to be a sign that a ghost has come to call. If this occurs during a seance held on Halloween night, it may be a sign that the spirits are angry or restless.

In the English community of East Anglia, Halloween was known as "Lating Night"—a term believed to derive from the word "latent," meaning that which is hidden or concealed.

On Lating Night, it was once customary in that part of the world for white candles to be lit just prior to the midnight hour and then carried throughout the fields and woodlands by brave villagers who were convinced beyond the shadow of a doubt that the Devil and his legion of demons freely roamed the land on this night of the year. The cloaked presence of evil was believed to be indicated by the flames of the candles sputtering, sparking, or dying out. However, if the flames of the candles burned in a manner that was steady and true, this meant that nothing wicked was afoot in that particular area.

Always burn new candles at Halloween to ensure the best of luck. Likewise, it is not a good idea to burn Halloween candles at any other time of the year. To do so may cause you to experience bad luck and/or strange happenings over which you will have no control.

Gazing into the flame of a candle on Halloween will enable you to peer into the future. Many Witches traditionally scry candle flames on Halloween to receive clairvoyant visions.

Omens can be read on Halloween by pouring the melted wax from a burning white candle into a cauldron filled with cold water and then interpreting the patterns formed by the wax as it cools.

It is said to be an omen of bad luck for a person to accidentally spill candle wax, or burn him or herself by wax or flame, on Halloween. To avert the misfortune, extinguish and relight the candle's flame nine consecutive times, each time repeating the following spoken charm:

ABRACADABRA
ABRACADAB
ABRACAD
ABRA
AB

BLOOD

If a person bleeds on Halloween, this is said to be a very grim omen. According to an ancient Anglo-Saxon belief, it supposedly indicates that he or she will not live to see the next Halloween. How this old superstition originated remains a mystery.

HAWTHORN

Unwise is the person who sits or sleeps beneath a hawthorn tree on Halloween, for on this day of the year when malevolent spirits roam the Earth, fairies are said to hide within hawthorns and cast their strange enchantments upon the mortals who unknowingly rest beneath these trees.

BLACK CAT

If a cat of the most sinister shade of black should cross your path on Halloween, this is said to be one of the most unluckiest omens you could ever receive. This superstitious belief, which is widespread throughout the United States, Spain, and Belgium, is less common in the British Isles where black cats have long been regarded as the harbingers of *good* luck.

FOOTSTEPS OF DEATH

If you should hear footsteps trailing close behind you on Halloween night, take care not to turn around to see who it is, for it may be Death himself! To look Death in the eye, according to ancient folklore the world over, is a sure way to hasten your own demise.

BORN ON HALLOWEEN

If a child is born on the last day of October, he or she will be gifted with the most remarkable of psychic powers, and be able to see, and converse with, the spirits of the dead. It is also said that those whose birthdays fall on Halloween can never be harmed by evil ghosts.

SHADOWS

Be warned that ill luck may knock upon your door if you are foolish enough to observe your own shadow in the moonlight on Halloween.

To cast a headless shadow or no shadow at all is still believed by many folks in the United States and Europe to be an omen of death in the course of the next year.

FIRE

According to an old English folk belief, you will invite bad luck into your home if you allow a fire to burn out on Halloween. Fires that burn out on New Year's Eve, Beltane (May 1st), Midsummer Eve, or Christmas Eve are believed to be equally as unlucky.

To remedy the situation, the fire must be rekindled by a lighted sod brought from the home of a priest.

THE DEAD

In many parts of the world, it is still believed that when the dark shadows of Halloween night begin to fall, the restless spirits of the dead find their way back to their earthly homes to warm themselves by the fire. And when the first rays of dawn streak across the sky, the spirits return to the realm of the dead for another year.

It is said that unwise is the one who tries to keep the dead from returning, for this is quite a dangerous thing to do. According to an old belief shared by many cultures, cursed are those who anger or interfere with the dead. Additionally, it is perilous for one to encounter a ghost face-to-face on Halloween.

THE DEVIL

It was once believed that if a person was brave enough to peer into a church window at the witching hour on Halloween, he or she would find the Devil at the pulpit, sur-

The Devil proclaims, "I am Pope."

rounded by an "unearthly light" and reading out the names of the sinners whose souls would belong to him before the next Halloween!

GOOD LUCK, BAD LUCK

It is believed that if a person lights a new orange-colored candle at midnight on Halloween and lets it burn until the sun rises, he or she will be the recipient of good luck. However, according to an old legend from Europe, any person who bakes bread or journeys after sunset on Halloween runs the risk of conjuring forth bad luck in great abundance.

HALLOWEEN MOON OMENS

If the moon at Halloween is new, this indicates that the coming year will be fertile ground for new beginnings to take place, such as the start of a new project, a new career, or even a new way of thinking. For those desiring children, a new moon at Halloween is a lucky omen, indicating a new birth within a year's time.

Good luck throughout the coming year is promised by a waxing Halloween moon. It also indicates growth and an increase of all things that are of a positive nature.

A full moon on Halloween night ensures that the powers of all forms of magick and divination practiced on this night will be at their greatest. A secret wish made at midnight will be realized within the coming year, and do not be surprised if an experience of a psychic nature awaits you in the very near future.

If Halloween night sees a waning moon, this can be an

An insight into the coming year can often be gained by the reading of omens found in the phase of the moon at Halloween.

omen of either good or bad consequences. It can indicate the elimination of such things as bad habits, unhealthy relationships, and obstacles within the coming year. Or it can point to a decrease (such as in one's health) or a loss of some kind soon to take place.

If what is known as the "dark phase of the moon" takes place on Halloween night, this is believed to be a very negative omen. Exercise extreme caution in all of your endeavors within the next twelve months, and it wouldn't hurt to protect yourself by wearing or carrying any type of amulet or talisman designed to ward off bad luck and misfortune.

Divinations and Incantations

The art and practice of Halloween divination is a tradition that dates back to the ancient Druids. On this night time and space are suspended, and our connection to the supernatural world is the strongest, allowing prophecy to take place. Halloween divination in various forms is still practiced today by a wide variety of cultures.

The most sacred of the eight Witches' Sabbats has long been regarded as the ideal time for engaging in all manners of psychic work. It is a mysterious night when Witches throughout the world clairvoyantly peer into the past, the present, and the future.

The traditional Halloween divination method favored by those who belong to the Craft is that of scrying (or gazing) into crystal balls, magick mirrors, and the flames of candles, cauldron fires, or outdoor bonfires. The term "scrying," derived from the old English word *descry,* means "to perceive from a distance; to discover by the eye." The divinatory use of crystals is said to date back to circa 1,000 B.C. Undeniably, it is one of the oldest forms of divination that continues to be practiced in modern times.

The proper method of scrying a crystal ball is as follows: Before consulting the crystal, allow yourself to enter into a meditative state. Focus your mind on a particular question or issue, and then gaze into the surface of the crystal ball. (You will most likely find that the best results are achieved when your scrying is performed in a darkened room with the bright light of a full moon, the gentle glow of a candle's flame, or some other light source that reflects off the crystal's surface.) In time, a vision should form. It may be an entire scenario or simply one or more symbols that will require interpretation on your part.

It is common for many crystal gazers to experience the formation of "clouds" within or around the crystal ball. The colors of the clouds and the directions in which they move are said to be highly significant. Traditionally, clouds that move to the right are considered to be a sign that a benign guiding spirit is present, but clouds that move to the left indicate that the spirit is unwilling or unable to offer guidance at the present time. Clouds that move in an upward direction indicate an affirmative answer to the scryer's question, while a negative reply is shown by clouds that move in a downward direction.

The color of the clouds also conveys meaning:

White clouds are believed to be favorable omens

Black ones are viewed as being unlucky

Red clouds, depending upon the scryer's personal interpretation, can either indicate a fiery, passionate love affair or serve as a warning of impending danger

Green clouds, a color associated with money, generally indicate an increase in riches, unless the clouds are seen moving in a downward (negative) direction.

Yellow clouds are said to indicate betrayal.

Blue clouds are signs of peace and tranquility.

Violet clouds indicate spiritual strength, psychic growth, and enlightenment.

Sometimes a crystal ball's clouds—regardless of their color—will gradually or suddenly yield to a clear vision of a future, present, or past event.

The art of crystal gazing (which is technically known as "crystalomancy") is one that requires a good deal of concentration and practice, and a novice scryer should not become discouraged if he or she does not achieve immediate results. As with any art, some people require more time to master the crystal ball, while others seem to be born with a natural flair for it.

Many crystal gazers ritually "recharge" their crystal balls once every month by placing them either on an outdoor altar or on a windowsill where they can absorb the rays of the full moon. Most keep their crystal balls covered by a black silk handkerchief when not in use, and don't allow anyone to handle their crystal balls, for they believe that this action disturbs or diminishes its occult vibrations, requiring it to be reconsecrated and recharged with the gazer's own psychic energy.

In addition to gazing into crystal balls, many Witches utilize the steady flame of a candle, a water-filled cauldron, or what are known as magick mirrors as a focus for their Halloween scrying rituals.

A magick mirror, also known as a Witch's looking glass, can be an ordinary mirror. However, most are typically made of dark polished stone, such as black obsidian, or fashioned from a slightly curved piece of glass with the concave side painted black. Many famous practitioners of the occult arts, such as John Dee, Count Alessandro Cagliostro, Agrippa, and Albertus Magnus, have been known to possess one. (John Dee, whose astrological and psychic services were provided to clients of nobility, utilized a black obsidian mirror he called a "shew stone." It is currently on display at the British Museum.)

The divinatory use of the magick mirror is a very old one, dating back to the time of the Roman Empire. The ancient Greeks and Italians, as well as the Magi of Persia were said to have been highly adept in magick mirror divination, employing it religiously.

To scry flames, cauldrons, magick mirrors, and other objects, follow the instructions previously given for working with a crystal ball.

Another popular method of Halloween divination used by many modern Witches is the pendulum. This divinatory device consists of a heavy object—often a quartz crystal or inverted brass pyramid—that is suspended from a long chain. (In the Middle Ages, women in Germany made pendulums by fastening a wedding band to a strand of their own hair. These simple, yet powerful, tools were often used in divinatory rituals concerning matters of love and marriage.) Other objects that have been used in the art of pendulum prediction include coins, keys, ancient relics, and gemstones.

Prior to using a pendulum for the first time, it is always a good idea to decide the sort of movement that will indicate affirmative and negative replies. Typically, a pendulum that swings in a clockwise circle or moves to the north and south indicates a "yes"; while one that swings in a counterclockwise circle or moves to the east and west indicates a "no."

Although affirmative and negative movements of the swinging pendulum may differ from one psychic to another, it is generally agreed upon that a pendulum that shows no movement of any kind after it has been asked a question indicates that a definite answer cannot be determined at that time, in which case the question should be asked again later. Sometimes the movement of the pendulum will appear confused or switch back and forth, and this usually is interpreted as a "maybe."

A good way to establish the meanings of the pendulum's movements is to ask it a question to which you already know the answer and then observe its movement. Hold the end of the pendulum's chain between the tips of your thumb and index finger, pose a question, and then wait for the pendulum to begin moving. In most cases, the pendulum will respond within one minute.

Some individuals feel that pendulum divination, a prognostication method dating back to before the birth of Christ, is simply achieved through the clairvoyant powers of the person who works the pendulum. However, others believe that the pendulum is actually set into motion by the diviner's spirit guides.

LOVE DIVINATION IN THE NEW WORLD

The tradition of foretelling the future and divining one's love life on Halloween originated long ago in Ireland, where the mysterious Druids lit sacred bonfires upon the hilltops and performed ancient divinatory rites at midnight on the 31st—the eve of Samhain.

From Ireland, the divinations and folk magick connected with Halloween spread to the British Isles, eventually making their way throughout Europe and accompanying immigrants across the ocean to the unfamiliar shores of North America and a new world that promised freedom and a better way of life.

In the United States—especially in the rural regions of New England—many young, unmarried women still retain two Halloween love traditions. The first calls for them to carry an oil-burning lamp or a candle-lit lantern to a spring of water and gaze into its depths at midnight. If done in complete silence, a reflection of their future husband is said to appear. If no such reflection occurs, this is an indication that marriage is not destined to take place within the course of the next year. Also, the divination should not be repeated until the following Halloween.

The second method popular among young ladies who desire to peek into the future and see what their husband-to-be and children will look like calls for the girl to go to a spring of water at sunrise on Halloween, carrying a glass containing a broken egg. A handful of the fresh water is poured into the glass, that the girl must then gaze into in complete silence. If she follows these instructions to the letter and if marriage and children are in her future, a vision of her family-to-be will soon appear within the egg-water mixture. As with the first method of divination, if no vision is seen, this means that marriage and children are not in the girl's future yet.

The old Halloween folk custom known as the "Church Porch Watch" was a widespread divinatory practice in Wales, as well as in the northern and western regions of England, up until the latter part of the nineteenth century.

At midnight on Halloween, those who desired to learn who in the village was destined to die within the coming year would gather in the church porch of their parish and wait there throughout the night, all the while keeping a watchful eye for the apparitions of those marked by Death to come and knock upon the door.

THROWING THE SHOE

The Irish have a simple method of divination known as "throwing the shoe." A person wishing to know his future removes one of his shoes on Halloween night and tosses it over the roof of his house. If the shoe lands pointing away from the house, this is a sign that the wearer will soon be traveling in that direction. If the shoe lands pointing toward the house, no travel is forecast within the coming year for the wearer. Good fortune is indicated if the shoe lands with the sole down. However, if it lands with the sole up, this is said to be a sign of impending misfortune or even death.

The divinatory practice of "throwing the shoe" is mentioned in the court records of a seventeenth-century Witchcraft trial held in the Orkney Islands of northeast Scotland: "Peter Holland's wife came to the said Helen, the said Peter being sick, and asked at her whether or not her husband would die or live. The said Helen commanded her to take his left foot shoe and cast it over the house, and said if the mouth of it fell up, he would live, and if down he would die."

Another Halloween divination involving footwear calls for a girl to remove both of her shoes upon retiring to bed on Halloween night and place them at right angles to one another to form the letter T. The following incantation must then be repeated:

> *I cross my shoes in the shape of a T,*
> *Hoping this night my true love to see,*
> *Not in his riches or his worst array,*
> *But in the clothes he wears every day.*

The apparition of the girl's future husband is then supposed to appear by her bedside or come into view if she looks over her right shoulder. Oftentimes, he will show himself to her in a dream. If no apparition appears, this indicates that she will not marry before the next Halloween.

DIVINATION WITH APPLES

To make a vision of your future husband appear over your shoulder as you gaze into a mirror, perform this divination on a Halloween night, alone in a room lit only by the soft glow of a candle. Cut an apple into nine pieces with a knife. (In occult tradition, nine is regarded as a highly magickal number.) Face a mirror as you eat the first eight pieces, and then spear the ninth one on the tip of the knife and hold it over your shoulder. According to legend, an apparition of your future husband will appear and take the ninth piece of the apple. However, if you wish to catch a glimpse of his face, you must take care not to take your eyes off the mirror, for his identity will only be revealed to you through his reflection in the glass. If you attempt to look directly at the apparition, you will see nothing.

To learn the initials of your future husband or wife, peel an apple in one long piece, and then toss the paring over your left shoulder or into a bowl of water. Turn around and look at the peel to see what form it has taken. If a letter of the alphabet, this is said to be an indication of your future spouse's first initial. Repeat the divination to obtain the initial of his or her last name. If the apple peel takes the form of a number, this is said to be an indication of his or her birthdate, or in some cases, the date on which you will meet or marry your spouse-to-be.

Another method calls for an apple peel to be hung on a nail by your front door. The initials of the first man who enters will be the same as those belonging to your future husband.

If you are a woman who is undecided between two suitors, perform the following divination on Halloween. Eat a red apple, and save two seeds from its core. Name them after the two men in your life, and then stick them on your forehead or one on each cheek, and wait to see which of the two drops off first. According to the divination, the man whom the remaining seed represents is the one you should marry for he will forever remain loyal to you.

To discover if your romantic partner's love for you is true, take an apple seed and name it after him or her. At the midnight hour on Halloween, cast the seed into a fire and recite the following magickal rhyme:

If thee loves me, pop and fly;
If thee fools me, lay and die.

If the apple seed emits a noise in bursting from the heat, this is said to be an indication of love. However, if the flames consume the seed without so much as the slightest crackle, the person named does not possess a true love for you.

The popular Halloween children's game known as "bobbing (or ducking) for apples" is actually a relic of an old Druidic divination rite known as Ordeal by Water. To play this "game," young gentlemen and ladies of unmarried status attempt to retrieve an apple from a number of apples floating in a large barrel or tub of water that is constantly stirred with a wooden stick (or some other equivalent of a Druidic wand). The trick is to pick up the apple by using only your teeth, and nothing else. Often, this is done with both hands tied or clasped behind the back, and sometimes with the players' eyes covered by a blindfold. A person who is successful in retrieving an apple in this fashion and who places the fruit beneath their pillow will receive visions of their future husband or wife as they sleep and dream on Halloween night.

In another version of Halloween apple divination, the names or initials of different eligible bachelors or bachelorettes are carved upon apples, which are then put into a barrel or tub of water. Players of the opposite sex, blind-

The apple has been used in divination rites since the days of the ancient Druids.

folded with hands clasped or tied behind their backs, proceed to "bob" for an apple. The apple that is successfully retrieved or bitten into reveals that person's future mate by the name or initials carved upon it.

A WELSH BONFIRE DIVINATION

In days of yore, it was a common practice in North Wales for families to take white stones—each one bearing the name of a different family member or a symbol marked to represent each person in the family—and cast them into a Halloween bonfire at the onset of the witching hour. On the morning of November 1, after the bonfire had died out, the ashes would be anxiously searched in the hopes of finding the white stones. It was believed that if any of the stones were missing, the persons whom they represented would die during the coming year.

HALLOWEEN FOOD DIVINATION

A method of love divination popular at Halloween parties in Scotland in the early twentieth century was to beat the following objects into a pot of mashed potatoes (or *champit taties*): a button, a thimble, and a ring. The lights in the room would then be turned off and boys and girls would each scoop out a bit of the mashed potatoes and eat it (carefully) in the dark. If a boy got the button, this was an indication that he would never take a wife. If a girl got the thimble, this meant that she was destined for spinsterhood. However, the ring was a sign of marriage and happiness in the future for whomever was lucky enough to get it.

In Ireland, a similar method of love divination traditionally performed on Halloween night called for a dish known as *colcannon* or *callcannon,* which was made up of mashed potatoes, parsnips, and chopped onions. Stirred into it was a ring, a coin, a thimble, and a small china doll.

The person who received the ring was believed to be the first to marry. The coin indicated wealth for the one who received it; the thimble indicated bachelorhood for a man and spinsterhood for a woman; and the china doll indicated that its recipient would be the first to have children.

Another Irish method involved a special cake known as a *Barmbrack,* within which was baked a ring. After the cake was removed from the oven and allowed to cool, it would be cut into slices and served to those who were unmarried.

Whoever received the slice containing the ring was believed to be the first to find a husband or a wife.

Occasionally, a nut would also be baked into the cake, and indicated marriage to a widow or widower. However, if the kernel of the nut was shriveled, this meant that wedding bells would never ring for the man or woman who picked the slice in which the nut was concealed.

PULLING THE KAIL

A Halloween method of love divination popular among the Irish and Scottish peasantry in the eighteenth and nineteenth centuries was known as "pulling the kail." It was carried out in the following manner: An unmarried woman, with her eyes shut or covered by a blindfold, would creep into a bachelor's garden (or kail yard) and, as the clock struck the witching hour of midnight, grasp at random for a stalk and pluck it from the earth.

According to folklore, the size, shape, and texture of the plant was able to reveal the appearance of the woman's future husband. If it was tall and straight, it was an indication that he would be strong and in good health. If it was shriveled, it meant he would be a sickly person. A well-grown stalk indicated that he would be a handsome man, while one that was crooked indicated marriage to a hunchback or a stingy man. A closed white stalk indicated an elderly mate, and an open green one meant a man who was younger. If any earth clung to the roots, this portended a man of great wealth, while roots that came out of the ground free of any dirt were indicative of precisely the opposite.

Even the way in which the heart of the stem tasted was

used to determine the natural temper and disposition of the future mate. For instance, one that tasted sweet and tender indicated a man who was kind and gentle, but one that possessed a sour or bitter taste pointed to a man whose disposition was disagreeable.

If the plant possessed any abnormalities, they were believed to reveal the same physical or mental traits of the future husband. For instance, if it had a club root, the future husband would be afflicted with a club foot, and so forth.

In England, a variation of this method called for an unmarried woman to go into a garden at midnight on Halloween and cut a cabbage. This supposedly invoked an apparition of her future husband. If no apparition appeared, this was taken as an indication of spinsterhood.

Cabbage stalk divinations were also performed by bachelors to find out if marriage was in the offing for them, and also to discover what their future wives would be like.

Cabbage stalks were once used by some Christians to discover whether a particular individual was destined to go to Heaven or Hell. Blindfolded, a person would pull up a cabbage at random, remove the blindfold, and then examine the stalk. If it was clean and light-colored, it indicated that he or she was reserved a place in Heaven. But if the cabbage was darkened by frost, it was taken as a sure sign that an eternity burning in the fires of Hell was the fate that awaited the individual after death.

THE WETTING OF THE SARK SLEEVE

The following divinatory practice for the lovelorn was once common in Ireland and Scotland. On Halloween night, a girl would go by herself to a south-flowing stream and dip the left sleeve of her sark (smock) three times into the cold water. (According to *Shetland Lore,* the water must be "where three lairds' lands meet.") This had to be done in complete silence, for it was believed that if any words were spoken during this divination, its magickal effects would be instantly broken. She would then return to her home and, exactly one hour before midnight, hang the sark up to dry before the kitchen fire. At eleven-thirty she had to turn the wet sleeve inside out, and then at the stroke of midnight, an apparition of her future husband would come down the chimney and turn the sleeve right again.

If the girl was able to keep herself from falling asleep, she could behold the face of her intended. However, if marriage was not in the girl's future, she would hear the sound of a bell ringing instead. (Note: For this "charm" to work, the door to the kitchen had to be set wide open.)

It is said that this old method of Halloween love divination evolved from an earlier Pagan rite dedicated to Freya, the blonde-haired, blue-eyed Norse goddess who presided over love and marriage.

THREE DISHES

The following method of love divination dates back to the Middle Ages and was a popular Halloween tradition in Ireland and Great Britain. Known in Scotland as "The Three Luggies," it involved three saucers (one containing clean water, the second containing foul water, and the third left empty), which would be set out on a table or arranged on the hearth. A man or woman was blindfolded and led to the saucers to dip his or her left hand into one of them.

If, by chance, the clean water was chosen, it signified that the blindfolded person would marry a young and attractive maiden or bachelor who had loved no other. The saucer containing the foul water signified marriage to a widow or widower, and in some traditions it was an indication that a woman was destined for widowhood. If the empty saucer was chosen, it signified, with equal certainty, that the future held no marriage at all. The divination was required to be carried out three times in a row, each time with the three saucers rearranged.

A variation on this method called for three dishes to be set out—one containing a piece of gold (signifying a rich marriage), another containing a ring (signifying an early marriage), and the third a thimble (signifying no marriage). In Victorian-era England, this old method of love divination was popular among children, who regarded it as a Halloween game.

A more macabre version of the old Halloween practice of revealing one's fate by the chance selection of a saucer was employed by the Irish. Every October 31, three saucers—one containing clean water, the second containing a bit of earth, and the third containing meal—would be arranged on the hearth. Blindfolded, a man or woman would touch at random one of the saucers, thus revealing his or her fate. If the saucer containing the clean water was chosen, it signified that he or she would live to see another Halloween. If the saucer with the soil was chosen, it signified that the man or woman would see the grave before the year came to a close. But lucky was the person who chose the saucer filled with meal, for this signified a long, happy life and the attainment of wealth.

DIVINING YOUR FUTURE HUSBAND'S TRADE

To discover the trade or occupation of their future husbands, young women in Scotland would perform the following divination on Halloween:

A woman would go to a field of barley and lay her head in the furrow between the third and fourth ridge. Whatever sound she heard supposedly indicated her future husband's trade. For instance, if she heard a hammering sound, this indicated that he would be a carpenter; the sound of cart wheels indicated a farmer; the sound of churchbells indicated a man of the cloth; and so forth.

Sometimes, instead of such a sound, a whispering voice emitted from the ground. If she listened with great care, it revealed what her future marriage mate did to make his living.

In some parts of the British Isles, this method of divination was traditionally performed on Midsummer Day instead of, or in addition to, Halloween, and utilized a hole dug at a spot where three or more roads intersected. However, for its magick to work, as with most Halloween divinations, it had to be carried out precisely at midnight and not one minute before or after the witching hour.

EGG DIVINATION

The practice of using eggs to determine one's future husband dates back to the Middle Ages and is believed to have originated in Ireland. It is performed in the following manner:

On Halloween, prepare a hardboiled egg and, after it has cooled to the touch, cut it in half with a sharp knife, while it is still in the shell. Remove the yolk from one half and fill the cavity with salt. Then eat that half of the egg, including the shell. Put the other half of the egg beneath your pillow while you recite the following incantation:

> *This egg I place beneath my head*
> *To dream of the living*
> *And not of the dead,*
> *To dream of the young man*
> *That I am to wed,*
> *Not in his apparel*
> *Nor in his array,*
> *But in the clothes*
> *That he wears every day.*

After reciting the rhyme, get into bed without speaking a word, taking care not to quench your thirst until the rising sun greets the new morning. If you follow these steps, supposedly you will dream about your future husband. However, if you dream that he is at hand with water, this is an indication that he will end up breaking off the engagement. It can also indicate that you will be deceived or disappointed in love.

In a similar method of love divination, a young woman or man is required to consume a raw or roasted salt herring and then recite an incantation similar to the one used in the egg divination prior to turning in for the night. If a marriage is destined, the future husband or wife will appear in a dream, offering a drink of water to quench the dreamer's thirst.

DUMB-CAKE

In the British Isles, one of the oldest and most popular methods of love divination to determine one's future husband was the Dumb-Cake. Although also performed at midnight on Christmas Eve, Saint Agnes' Eve, and Midsummer Eve, the Dumb-Cake divination is associated mainly with Halloween.

Numerous recipes exist for Dumb-Cake, although it generally consists of simple ingredients. One recipe for Dumb-Cake calls for "an egg-shell-full of salt, an egg-shell-full of wheat meal, and an egg-shell-full of barley-meal." Another recipe requires equal parts flour and salt, with a bit of water added; while another calls for flour, salt, and an egg which is blown upon three times. A Dumb-Cake made of soot is mentioned in the seventeenth-century work, *Satan's Invisible World Discovered* by G. Sinclair.

Traditionally, the cake batter is prepared and poured on a hot griddle by an unmarried woman whose virginity remains intact. After the cake is cooked broad and thin, she must break off one piece and eat it, then walk backward to her bed and place the rest of the cake beneath her pillow. If she does all of this in serious silence without uttering one single word or even smiling, the Dumb-Cake will invoke a pleasant dream in which her future love mate will manifest.

In some parts of the British Isles, the Dumb-Cake is still used to determine the initials of a woman's future husband.

The procedure for this is the same as previously outlined. However, the woman must first take a pin and trace her own initials on the top of the cake before baking it. In the morning, the cake is carefully examined for the initials of her future husband, traced on the cake during the night by his apparition.

GARTER AND KNOTS

To make your future husband appear to you in a dream, an old method of love divination from Scotland calls for three knots to be tied on a left leg garter on Halloween. As each knot is tied, the following incantation should be recited:

> *This knot, this knot I knit*
> *To see the thing I never saw yet . . .*
> *To see my love in his array,*
> *And what he walks in every day;*
> *And what his occupation be,*
> *This night I in my sleep may see.*
> *And if my love be clad in green,*
> *His love for me is well seen;*
> *And if my love is clad in gray,*
> *His love for me is far away;*
> *But if my love be clad in blue,*
> *His love for me is very true.*

After reciting the incantation (some traditions require that it be spoken thrice), place the knotted garter beneath your pillow and then go to sleep and dream.

According to tradition, for this divination to work properly it must be performed without speaking a single word to anyone, and the woman must sleep in a county other than that in which she lives.

A similar method practiced long ago by bachelors in South Wales calls for nine knots to be tied on a garter, which is then tied to the bedpost. After walking backward to bed, undressing only with his left hand, and then placing his shoes beneath his pillow, the following incantation is repeated three times to induce a divinatory dream of his future mate:

> *I do this for to see*
> *Who my future wife shall be,*
> *Where she is and what she wears.*

In some versions of this divination, the garter is tied nine times around the bedpost after being knotted nine times, and then the following rhyme is spoken:

> *This knot I knit,*
> *This knot I tie,*
> *To see my love as he/she goes by*
> *In his/her apparel and array*
> *As he/she walks in every day.*

ASH DIVINATION

To determine their future wife, bachelors in Ireland, the Isle of Man, and Lancashire (England) used to scatter ashes in a quiet lane at Halloween. They would then wait anxiously to see which young lady followed the trail first. The one who did was believed to be the future spouse.

IVY LEAF DIVINATION

To discover if any member of the family is destined to die during the coming year, an English method of divination calls for the name of each person to be written upon ivy leaves—each leaf bearing a different name. On Halloween night, the leaves are placed in a bowl of water, and then inspected the following morning. If one is found shriveled, turned black, or with the symbol of a coffin marked upon it, this is said to be an omen of death for the person whose name is on that leaf. A leaf with black spots indicates sickness, but one with red spots means a violent death unless a "wise man" can grant protection through the recitation of special incantations and other magickal skills.

Ivy leaves have also been used to induce dreams in which future lovers appear. To do this, simply place ten ivy leaves beneath your pillow before you go to bed on Halloween night.

Sacred to the ancient Roman god Bacchus, and believed to offer protection against all forms of evil, the ivy is a plant that has long been connected to the art and practice of divination.

WALNUT TREE DIVINATION

The walnut is a tree that has been connected to the world of love and romance since the days of the Roman Empire, and possibly before. It has long been used by women and men in many parts of the world for divining future love affairs.

One popular method calls for a person to walk clockwise three times around a walnut tree at the midnight hour on Halloween, gaze up into the branches, and then politely ask the tree for some walnuts. The face of their future husband or wife will materialize at once.

It is also believed that if an individual should fall asleep under a walnut tree, he or she will see the face of a future spouse in a dream. However, according to occult folklore, falling asleep under a walnut tree may bring on a dangerous sleep-enchantment from which there is no waking up. Perhaps this explains why the walnut tree has acquired the curious and ominous nickname, the tree of evil.

DIVINATION BY LEAD

On Halloween night, fill an old spoon with scraps of lead and then hold it over the flame of a new white candle until the lead is completely melted. Pour it into a pail of cold water, and the shape it assumes after it cools will reveal the trade of your future husband. For instance, if it takes on the appearance of a ship, this indicates that he will be a sailor; a book indicates a teacher; a lancet a doctor; and so forth.

THE TRAIL OF THE SNAIL

A rather unusual method of love divination, dating back to Ireland in the Middle Ages, calls for a black snail to be placed upon a flour-covered dinner plate or tossed over your shoulder on to an ash-covered hearth at the midnight hour on Halloween. (In some traditions, the snail is placed on a flour-covered plate and then baked alive in an oven.)

In the morning, the snail's slimy trail among the flour or the ashes is believed to reveal the initials of your future husband or wife's name.

DIVINATION BY OATS

To find out how many children you will have, pluck a stalk of oats on Halloween. The number of grains attached to the stalk will correspond to the number of children. However, if the top grain is missing, this is said to be an indication for a woman that she will lose her virginity before her wedding day.

The art and practice of divination by oats was at one time a popular Halloween tradition in the country of Scotland. Like many of the other amatory fortune-telling methods associated with the old Druid's New Year, it is centuries old.

WINDING THE YARN

Several old methods of love divination utilized a ball of yarn to make the apparition of a future spouse appear. Some traditions required that the yarn be of the color blue.

One method called for the ball of yarn to be thrown out of a window at midnight on Halloween, and then wound in on a reel from within while the diviner repeats the paternoster (the Lord's Prayer) backwards. Another called for the yarn to be thrown into a lime kiln and then wound up until "invisible hands" caught the thread. The question: "Who pulls my yarn?" would be asked aloud, and a voice would reply by naming the future husband or wife, or an apparition of the future spouse would materialize. This divination was performed alone at the witching hour and otherwise in complete silence.

If no reply was received and if no apparition appeared, this indicated that marriage was not in the future. Spinsterhood or bachelorhood was also foretold if, while the yarn was being wound up, nothing took hold of it. If the thread broke while being reeled in, this was a bad omen. Some believed it portended poverty or bad luck, while others believed it indicated a broken marriage engagement.

WINNOWING THE CORN

Country-folk in Ireland and in various agricultural regions throughout the British Isles once believed that if an unmarried woman went into a barn at midnight on Halloween and thrice used a riddle to separate grain from chaff, or, according to the poet Robert Burns, took the "instrument used in winnowing the corn" and went "through all the attitudes of letting down corn against the wind," an apparition of her future husband would materialize. If, however, the image of a coffin appeared to her at any time during the divination, this was a grim omen that she would be in her grave within the next twelve months!

Additionally, there appears to be an element of danger attached to this method of divination. Burns warned that the barn doors should be thrown wide open, or better yet removed from their hinges, prior to winnowing the corn. This precautionary measure was necessary because there existed the possibility that the apparition summoned by this charm may trap the seeker in the barn and, in Burns' words, "do you some mischief."

BURNING THE NUTS

In the British Isles, nuts have played such a major role in Halloween divination that the 31st of October came to be known there as "Nutcrack Night." Symbolizing life and fertility, nuts were, and still are, used in many parts of England, Scotland, and Ireland to predict a young man's or woman's love life.

One popular method, known in Ireland as "To Burn Their Nits," calls for two nuts to be named after a man and a

Nut divination being performed on Halloween night. In the British Isles it was so popular that October 31 came to be known as "Nutcrack Night."

woman who are in love with each other and then to be placed side by side on the hearth. A happy marriage within the year is indicated for the couple is both nuts burn quietly to ashes together. However, if one of the nuts crackles, springs apart or jumps into the flames, it indicates that the lover whom the nut represents will be untrue. But if both nuts crackle, spring apart or jump into the flames, it means that quarrels will ensue, causing the lovers to go their separate ways.

If a girl had two sweethearts and desired to learn which one would be more faithful to her, all she needed to do (according to an old Irish custom) was to write her name or initials upon a nut, her first sweetheart's name or initials upon a second nut, and her other sweetheart's name or initials upon a third nut. All three nuts should then be placed upon the hearth and their behavior closely observed. The more faithful lover would be indicated by whichever nut burned more steadily with hers.

Another version of Halloween nut divination calls for nuts (particularly hazelnuts) to be named for each person present, and then cast into a fire to roast. Whichever nut jumped first indicated that the person whose name was upon it would be the first to leave home. (Nuts that popped out of the grate also indicated travel in the near future.) Nuts that burned quietly indicated an "even and uneventful" life.

Sometimes a secret wish would be made prior to a nut being cast into the fire. If it burned up quickly, this meant that the wish would come true. But if it took the nut a long time to burn, or if it did not catch flame at all, this meant that the person would not get his or her wish.

To learn if someone's love for you is true, place a nut in the fire or upon the bars of the grate, and then recite the following incantation:

If (name) *loves me, pop and fly,*
If (name) *hates me, lie and die.*

A Welsh method of nut divination is as follows: Place a nut on the hearth at midnight on Halloween. If it blazes brightly, this is a sure sign of prosperity within the coming year. But if it should smolder or pop, expect to receive misfortune in the very near future.

HEMP SEED DIVINATION

At midnight on Halloween, go alone into the fields or a garden with a handful of hemp seeds. Scatter them in the dark, or toss them over your right shoulder, as you recite the following divinatory incantation:

Hemp seed, I saw thee,
Hemp seed, I saw thee,
And him (or *her*) *that is to be my true love*
Come after me and draw thee.

Another incantation is as follows:

Hemp seed I sow;
Hemp seed, grow;
He (or *She*) *that is my true love*
Come after me and mow.

In some traditions, the last line of the incantation is: "Come after me and pou thee" or "Come after me in shaw thee" (which means, to show thyself). Others add the following lines:

> *Not in his* (or *her*) *best*
> *Or Sunday array,*
> *But in the clothes*
> *He* (or *she*) *wears every day.*

You may have to repeat the incantation several times (some traditions call for it to be spoken nine times), but eventually the invoked apparition of your future spouse will appear behind you with a scythe to reap the magickally-grown hemp. To see his or her face, you must—without fear in your heart—look over your left shoulder.

The Witches' Sabbat

In the Middle Ages, Halloween was referred to as the "Black Sabbath" by churchmen who firmly believed, and devoted a major part of their lives and religious careers to making the masses believe, that Witches celebrated Halloween by sacrificing and cannibalizing children, dining on bread made from human feces and urine, kissing the backsides of goats and black cats, copulating with the Devil, and other atrocities.

These bizarre acts, and many others, were said to take place each year at the midnight hour on Halloween Eve. They were also said to be held at a secret location where broomstick-riding Witches and Warlocks gathered in the nude to pay homage to the Lord of Hell, stir up vile potions in their cauldrons, and use their knowledge of the forbidden arts of sorcery to make life as miserable as possible for all of the God-fearing Christian folk.

According to Rossell H. Robbins's *The Encyclopedia of Witchcraft and Demonology,* the investigators and judges connected with the Inquisition appear to be largely responsible for fabricating the conception of the Witches' Sabbat and its celebration of diabolical rites during the fourteenth and fifteenth centuries. By the sixteenth century, the Sabbat was an established part of belief in witchcraft throughout most of the European countries.

It is believed that the link between the word "Sabbat" (Hebrew for the seventh day) and the seasonal gatherings of Witches was forged by the early church. Pagan folks who remained true to the Old Religion (as well as those who were Jews and Mohammedans) were branded by the Church as "traitors to God" and made targets for Christian opposition. Interestingly, in early works, even the word "synagoga" from "synagogue" was used by the Church to mean the Witches' Sabbat or Black Mass.

It is doubtful that the above-mentioned practices associated with the Witches' Sabbat actually took place at any location outside of the minds of those possessing overactive, if not twisted, imaginations! In the interest of dispelling the many die-hard myths, misconceptions, and stereotypes that are connected to Witches and their celebration of Halloween, it seems only appropriate to discuss the ways that Witches do *not* celebrate it.

First and foremost, Witches do not believe in or worship the Christian Devil. He plays no role whatsoever in contemporary Witchcraft, Wicca, and Paganism (which is often referred to as Neo-Pagnism). Therefore, the Devil is not incorporated into the celebration of Halloween as a Sabbat in any way. Witches do not offer prayers, libations, or sacrifices to him, sign pacts in blood with him, sell their souls to him, involve or invoke him in any aspect of their spirituality or magickal practices, or even acknowledge his existence outside of symbolism and mythology.

Witches making merry at the Sabbat.

Witches do not perform human or animal sacrifices at Sabbats, or for the sake of any spell or ritual. The Goddess and the Horned God—the two central deities worshipped and invoked by most who follow the path of Wicca—do not thirst for blood or hunger for the souls of sacrificial victims. Witches also do not feast upon human flesh, nor do they dine on cakes, breads, and any other food made with the feces, urine, or blood of humans or animals.

Witches, of course, never actually flew on broomsticks, although they may have used them as a safe substitute for a magic wand during the Burning Times, as brooms were a necessity in every kitchen. Brooms (or "besoms," as many Witches call them) are generally reserved for handfasting ceremonies where couples traditionally "jump the broom" for good luck and fertility (as an obvious phallic symbol), or for use within the ritual circle as a tool to symbolically sweep away negative energy vibrations. Flying ointments containing herbs with poisonous or hallucinogenic properties are not used, and Black Magick is never performed.

Lastly, Sabbat orgies are not engaged in by the average modern Witch, although it is not an uncommon practice for many Wiccan traditions to perform their rites and celebrate their Sabbats skyclad (a word used by Witches to mean "in the nude"). The Great Rite (a Wiccan ritual involving sexual intercourse between the High Priestess and High Priest of a coven) is performed at certain Sabbats; however, not all covens incorporate this intimate ritual into their religious practices.

So, what does the Sabbat of Halloween mean then to modern Witches? And how do they celebrate it? Halloween is one of the four major Sabbats celebrated by the modern Witch, and it is by far the most popular and important of the eight that are observed within the course of a year. It is a point in time which marks both the end and the beginning of the Wheel of the Year, and is a night devoted to honoring all spirits of departed loved ones. Witches regard Halloween as their New Year's Eve, celebrating it with sacred rituals, feasts consisting of traditional Pagan foods, song, and dance, and plenty of old-fashioned merry-making. Many strive to keep alive the old Pagan customs associated with Halloween, while others delight in incorporating new traditions into their Sabbat celebrations and observances. It is also common for spells designed to banish weaknesses to be cast at this time of the year.

The art and practice of divination (especially in the form of scrying) is traditionally performed at Halloween by many Witches throughout the United States, Canada, and Europe. Additionally, it is customary for covens and solitary practitioners alike to leave offerings of food for the souls of the dead outside at night after performing their rituals.

Apples have long been considered one of the foods of the dead and have played a major role in the Halloween love divination rituals of yesteryear. They have been utilized in a variety of ways to determine future mates and even to make apparitions of them appear. In certain traditions of Wicca, the apple symbolizes the human soul. On Halloween, many Wiccans ritually bury apples in the soil of Mother Earth to honor and nourish the souls of the dead who are believed to be reborn when the Spring Equinox arrives.

Other Wiccan activities associated with Halloween include meditation, past-life regression, the drying of herbs for the coming winter months, and communing with the dead.

At Halloween, many Wiccan traditions pay homage to the Dark Lord or Holly King aspect of the Horned God (the masculine personification of the Life Force); who dies each year on this night and goes forth into the Underworld. There, He assists the passing of souls in and out of that realm and waits for His own rebirth to occur.

At the Sabbat of Yule, which occurs annually on the Winter Solstice, He is once again born to the Goddess, and becomes the Bright Lord or the Oak King. He remains in this aspect until the arrival of the Summer Solstice when He impregnates the same Goddess who bore Him, and once again becomes the Dark Lord or Holly King. At Halloween,

A fifteenth-century illustration of a Witch riding a goat to the Sabbat.

the Horned God is sometimes called the King of Shadows.

His annual death is part of an eight-fold cycle corresponding to the eight Sabbats of the Wheel of the Year, and is a self-sacrifice necessary for the salvation of His people.

The traditional candle colors used in Halloween spells and Sabbat rites are black and orange, and the sacred gemstones of this Sabbat are carnelian and all black gemstones, especially jet, obsidian, and onyx. They are often worn in the form of rings, pendants, and other magickal jewelry. Sometimes they are placed at the four directional points along the circle, or used in various ways in Halloween spells and divinations.

The following items are used by many Witches as Halloween altar decorations: jack-o'-lanterns, pumpkins, turnips, apples, photographs of deceased family members and friends, crystal balls and other tools of divination, a small statue representing the Goddess in Her aspect of the Crone, nuts, autumn leaves, and baskets or small cauldrons filled with mugwort and other herbs that correspond to this Sabbat and the season. In addition, Halloween candles—either store-bought or hand-crafted, and in the shapes of traditional symbols of this holiday—can often be found illuminating the altars and ritual circles of contemporary Witches and Pagans on October 31.

HALLOWEEN SABBAT RITUAL FOR COVENS AND SOLITARIES

Traditionally, Halloween (or Samhain) Sabbat rituals are performed on the night of October 31 at the witching hour of midnight. Sabbat celebrations often last until the rising of the sun on November 1.

The following Sabbat ritual is designed for use either by covens or solitary practitioners of the Craft. (To adapt it for solitaries, simply change some of the words in the spoken parts of the rituals such as "we" to "I", and so forth.) This is a basic Witches' ritual and it can be modified to suit the needs of any particular Wiccan or Pagan tradition. Each step of the ritual is explained in detail so that those who are new to the practice of Wicca can gain a better understanding of the ways of the Craft.

Altar set-up

Before performing this ritual, erect an altar, either indoors or out, and upon it arrange the following ritual items in the manner prescribed: Two black candles (one to represent the Goddess in Her aspect of Crone or Lady of Darkness, and the other to represent the Horned God in His aspect of Lord of Shadows) should be placed upon the altar—one at each side. Some traditions prefer to use white candles to represent the deities; others employ silver candles for the Goddess, and gold ones for Her horned consort. Use whichever works best for you.

In the center of the altar, arrange a black cast iron cauldron to be used later in a "sacrificial" fire rite. (This does not involve the harming of life in any way. The rite is a sacrifice in the sense that you are ending something negative in order for positive growth and changes to occur. More on this later.) The cauldron will be filled with a bit of cauldron spirit (rubbing alcohol) and then set ablaze, so make sure that it is placed securely upon a cast iron base, or some other type of fireproof stand. (In most cases, an ordinary brick will do just fine.)

To either side of the cauldron, place the rubbing alcohol and a book of matches. Most Witches prefer lighting their cauldrons, candles, and incense with matches rather than with cigarette lighters because sulfur (once known as "brimstone") has been believed since the Middle Ages to possess the power of purification. In front of the cauldron, place rolled-up slips of parchment upon which all persons attending the rite have written down the negative things in their lives they wish to "sacrifice". Also on the altar, place an apple, a skull- or ghost-shaped candle to represent the spirits of the dead, a small bowl of salt, a small bowl of water, an altar bell, an incense burner filled with sage or sage incense, and an athame. (An athame is a ritual dagger possessing a double-edged blade and a black handle. It symbolizes the masculine aspect and is used for drawing the circle and for storing and directing magickal energy.)

You may also decorate your altar with autumn leaves, herbs, photographs of deceased loved ones, and anything else that you consider sacred or has special significance to you. Many modern Witches and Pagans feel that a Halloween altar would not be complete without a grinning jack-o'-lantern casting its eerie candlelit glow.

Some Wiccan traditions prefer being skyclad (without clothing) when performing rituals, as they feel that nudity enhances their magickal energies and "equalizes" all members of a coven. However, there are many Wiccans who prefer to wear robes when performing rites and working their magick. The choice is strictly up to the individual coven or solitary practitioner.

The Ceremony

Begin the ceremony by lighting the sage or incense and the two altar candles. The High Priestess invokes the four elements of Earth, Air, Fire, and Water in the following manner. Face north, and say:

> *We call to thee*
> *O ancient spirits of the element earth*
> *And guardians of the northern sphere.*
> *Tonight we seek thy presence here*
> *In this circle and in our hearts*
> *That beat as one.*

Come, elementals, come. We beseech thee.
Bring forth thy strength,
Stability, and magick.
Partake of this sabbat rite
And blessed be!

Turn to the east, and say:

We call to thee
O ancient spirits of the element air
And guardians of the eastern sphere.
Tonight we seek thy presence here
In this circle and in our hearts
That beat as one.
Come, elementals, come. We beseech thee.
Bring forth thy wisdom,
Dreams, and creativity.
Partake of this sabbat rite
And blessed be!

Turn to the south, and say:

We call to thee
O ancient spirits of the element fire
And guardians of the southern sphere.
Tonight we seek thy presence here
In this circle and in our hearts
That beat as one.
Come, elementals, come. We beseech thee.
Bring forth thy warmth,
Energy, and flames of passion.

> *Partake of this sabbat rite*
> *And blessed be!*

Turn to the west, and say:

> *We call to thee*
> *O ancient spirits of the element water*
> *And guardians of the western sphere.*
> *Tonight we seek thy presence here*
> *In this circle and in our hearts*
> *That beat as one.*
> *Come, elementals, come. We beseech thee.*
> *Bring forth thy love,*
> *Intuition, and power to cleanse.*
> *Partake of this sabbat rite*
> *And blessed be!*

Pour the salt into the bowl of water and stir it, using the tip of the athame's blade. Take the ritual dagger in your "power hand" (the hand you normally use for writing) and the bowl of saltwater in the other, and cast the circle by starting in the north (the direction traditionally associated with enchantments, earth mysteries, and fairy folk) walking in a clockwise fashion. As you do this, dip the blade into the saltwater and sprinkle the boundary of the circle, and say:

> *I now conjure and proclaim this to be a circle of*
> *power, and a sacred space between the worlds of the*
> *visible and the invisible, the worlds of light and*
> *shadow, the worlds of mortal and spirit immortal.*

Sabbat moon of enchantment, guide us well and shine your light of Hecate's blessings down upon this pagan rite. Let the wisdom of the Crone Goddess flow through us like blood through veins. Let Her magick weave us a web of dreams to follow in our hearts. Let Her strength and stability fill us, nourish us, heal, and sustain us, and let the divine energies of the Horned God, who reigns tonight as the dark lord, the lord of shadows, strengthen us and bless us with power and balance. Let His ancient ways dwell within our hearts.

Return the athame and bowl of saltwater to the altar. The circle has now been cast and consecrated, creating a sacred space. Ring the altar bell three times, and say:

> *Hail to the four elements,*
> *Ancient and mystical,*
> *Powerful and eternal.*
> *Welcome Lord of Shadows*
> *And Lady of Darkness to this rite!*
> *With sacred bell and witch's blade,*
> *Rising smoke and dancing flame*
> *We honor thee on this night*
> *And open our hearts to your magick*
> *Spell of earth, moon, sun, and stars.*
> *We are truly blessed by your presence,*
> *By your love and protection,*
> *And by your guidance.*
> *We now become as one*
> *With our beloved Goddess and God*

In perfect love and in perfect trust.
As it is willed, so mote it be!

All members of the coven should now raise their palms to the sky, and say:

So mote it be!

Take the incense burner and smudge yourself with the smoke of the smoldering sage. Offer it to the covener to your left, and as the incense burner is passed clockwise around the circle, repeat the following words:

On this night of shadows, when the old ones in their darkest aspects reign supreme, we gather in this circle and open our bodies, our minds, and our spirits to the witching hour.

The season of the Witch now casts its spell upon us, drawing us into its shadow-enshrouded mysteries, its macabre beauty, and its ancient magick that will for-ever endure.

Return the incense burner to the altar. Light the skull- or ghost-shaped candle with a match, raise up your arms in a traditional Witch's prayer position with the palms of your hands turned up, and say:

We light this candle of death in honor of those whose physical bodies have returned to the dark womb of our sacred mother earth. Tonight from their graves they rise. Tonight their spirits shall roam unchained through this world of flesh and blood until the rising of the newborn sun.

Thin grows the veil that separates the worlds of the living and the dead. Tonight the doors to the ghostly realms beyond stand open. Behold the spirits, phantoms, ghosts, and pale specters that go drifting by upon the wind.

We call to thee now, o spirit/s of (name/s). Our circle is open to you should you choose to come. We invite you to join us as we celebrate this sacred rite, and we welcome you with perfect love and perfect trust, free of fear, sorrow or hesitation. Come, loved ones, come, and be with us here and now.

Note: In regards to communion with the dead, spirits should always be invited to a Sabbat rite, and never summoned in the way that ceremonial magicians of old once demanded demons and other entities to manifest themselves. If the spirits do return to the world of the living at Halloween to partake of the loving energies and celebration of the Sabbat, it should be of their own free will. Most Wiccans and modern day Witches and Pagans do not feel that it is ethical to "call back" the dead.

All members of the coven should now devote a few minutes to thinking fond thoughts about their deceased loved ones. If personal prayers are desired, let them now be spoken.

Take the athame in your power hand, and the apple in your other. With the tip of the blade, draw the sacred symbol of the pentagram (five-pointed star) in the air above the apple, and say:

> *We call upon thee,*
> *Lord of Shadows*
> *And Lady of Darkness*
> *To bless this apple*
> *To be the food for the dead.*
> *Let any and all visitors*
> *From the otherworld of spirit*
> *Find sustenance in this fruit*
> *As they pass from this world*
> *To the next. So mote it be!*

All members of the coven should now say in unison:

> *So mote it be!*

Return the apple and athame to the altar, and say:

> *And just as life itself is a neverending cycle of birth, death, and rebirth, the wheel of the year has once again turned, bringing us an ending and a new beginning. The time has come for us to honor the memory of those who have crossed over to the other side.*
>
> *And at this final phase of the eight-fold solar cycle, we must ready ourselves to release the past and to look*

*beyond this dimension of time and space to gain in-
sight of the things yet to be.*

The time has now come for the High Priestess to light
the cauldron of endings and new beginnings.

Pour some rubbing alcohol (about one-quarter cup) into
the cauldron and light it by carefully dropping in a lit match.
The cauldron should immediately begin to blaze. (**Warning:**
Make sure before lighting the cauldron that it is resting securely upon a fireproof stand and is not close to any flamma-
ble substances or things that can easily catch on fire, such as
drapes. Do not touch the cauldron while it is hot unless you
cover your hands with protective oven mitts. If the fire must
be extinguished before it burns itself out, smother it by cover-
ing the cauldron with a lid, or by sprinkling salt or sand over
the flames. Do not pour cold water on to or in to the hot
cauldron, otherwise it may crack. And remember, whenever
you are working with the element of Fire use caution and
common sense, and always respect the spirits of the flame!)

Take the slips of parchment upon which are written the
"sacrifices" and cast them into the cauldron's fire. As you do
this, all members of the coven should repeat the following
incantation in unison:

> *Air and fire, water and earth,*
> *Cauldron of death that brings rebirth,*
> *Into thy flames we cast our tokens*
> *To attain our goals unspoken.*
> *Help our faults and weaknesses vanish,*
> *Let our negative traits be banished.*

Burn and blaze! Burn and blaze!
Magickal power we do raise;
Ancient ways and Gods we praise;
Into the future now we gaze.

All members of the coven should now join hands to form a human circle around the flaming cauldron, and then gaze silently into the dancing flames, inviting clairvoyant visions to appear in the mind's eye.

The coven should continue the divination until the flames have all died out. If desired, more rubbing alcohol may be added to the cauldron and lit with a match so that the time for fire scrying can be lengthened. Whatever visions or feelings perceived should be shared by all after the close of the ritual, unless the coven members agree beforehand to do otherwise.

Closing the Ceremony

After the fire-scrying phase of the ritual has been completed, it is now time to bring the Sabbat rite to a close. However, before the circle is uncast, the invoked deities and the four elements must be thanked and then bidden farewell. The High Priestess should face the altar and raise her arms up in a traditional Witch's prayer position, and say:

O Lady of Darkness
And Lord of Shadows,
We offer thee our love and thanks
For attending this sabbat rite

And for empowering our magick.
O ancient ones, we bid thee farewell.
Blessed be, and so mote it be!

All members of the coven should now say in unison:

Blessed be, and so mote it be!

Once again, take the athame in your power hand. Face the direction of west, and say:

With love do we now
Give thanks and bid farewell
To the guardians of the west
Whose magick is the element of water.
Return now in peace, harming none,
To thy place in nature.
Blessed be!

All members of the coven should now say in unison:

Blessed be!

Face the direction of south, and say:

With love do we now
Give thanks and bid farewell
To the guardians of the south
Whose magick is the element of fire.
Return now in peace, harming none,

To thy place in nature.
Blessed be!

All members of the coven should now say in unison:

Blessed be!

Face the direction of east, and say:

With love do we now
Give thanks and bid farewell
To the guardians of the east
Whose magick is the element of air.
Return now in peace, harming none,
To thy place in nature.
Blessed be!

All members of the coven should now say in unison:

Blessed be!

Face the direction of north, and say:

With love do we now
Give thanks and bid farewell
To the guardians of the north
Whose magick is the element of earth.
Return now in peace, harming none,
To thy place in nature.
Blessed be!

All members of the coven should now say in unison:

Blessed be!

Holding the athame, uncast the circle in the opposite manner in which it was first cast: Start at the north and walk counterclockwise. As you do this, say the following words:

This circle is now uncast
And this pagan rite concluded.
Merry we meet, merry we part,
And merry shall we meet again.
A happy Halloween
And a joyous new year to one and all!
And as it is willed, so mote it be!

It is a tradition among many covens for its members to warmly embrace one another and exchange blessings after a ritual.

Extinguish the candles on the altar either by using a candle snuffer or pinching out the flames with your moistened fingertips. (Many Pagan folks believe that using your breath to blow out the flames of ritual candles brings bad luck, insults the gods, and/or symbolically "blows away" all of your magick.)

Remove the apple from the altar and bury it in the soil of Mother Earth to nourish the souls of the dead on this very special night of the year.

Notes

1. Should you feel it necessary to make any changes or additions to this ritual, please feel free to do so. The more

you personalize your magickal Craft, the better the results shall be for you. And always keep in mind that although words possess great power, the words you recite in an incantation, prayer, or chant are not nearly as important as the intent that lies behind them.

2. Some Wiccan traditions perform what is known as "The Great Rite" during their ritual observance of the Halloween Sabbat. This is an act of ritual sexual intercourse between a coven's High Priestess and High Priest, which is normally carried out in private. In addition to raising magickal energy, it represents the sacred union of the Goddess and Her consort, the Horned God. Many Wiccans who incorporate the Great Rite into their Sabbat rituals do so in a strictly nonsexual, symbolic fashion with the High Priest dipping the blade of his athame (male/yang symbol) into the wine-filled chalice (female/yin symbol) of the High Priestess while reciting special prayers. In addition, some Wiccan traditions end their Sabbat rituals and esbats (monthly full or new moon coven meetings) with what is called a Cakes and Wine (or Cakes and Ale) Ceremony. According to Scott Cunningham's *Living Wicca*, the purpose of this "rite-within-a-rite" is to ground energy and create a direct link between Wiccan practitioner and his or her deities.

3. The following is a list of Pagan gods and goddesses from various pantheons around the world. Each one is connected, in one way or another, to Halloween/Samhain:

Pagan Gods

Am-Heh (Egyptian), Arawn (Welsh), Corn Father (Native American), Coyote Brother (Native American), Dagda (Irish), Dis (Roman), Eite-Ade (Etruscan), Ghede (Voodoo loa), Hades (Greek), Heimdall (Norse), Kronos or Cronus (Greco-Phoenician), Loki (Norse), Maderha (Lapp), Nefertum (Egyptian), Odin (Norse), Pluto (Greco-Roman), Rangi (Maori), Samana (Aryan), Sekmhet (Egyptian), Woden (Teutonic), and Xocatl (Aztec).

Pagan Goddesses

The following is a list of Pagan goddesses from various pantheons around the world. Each one of these ancient deities is connected, in one way or another, to Halloween/Samhain:

Al-Ilat (Persian), Baba Yaga (Russian), Babd (Irish), Bastet or Pasht (Egyptian), Bebhionn (Irish), Bronach (Irish), Brunhilde (Teutonic), Caillech or Cailleac (Irish/Scottish), Carlin (Scottish), Cassandra (Greek), Cerridwen (Welsh/Scottish), Crobh Dearg (Irish), Devanyani (Indian), Dolya (Russian), Edda (Norse), Elli (Teutonic), Eris (Greek), Fortuna (Greco-Roman), Frau Holde (Teutonic), Frigga (Norse), Hakea (Polynesian), Hecate (Greek), Hel (Norse), Husbishag (Semitic), Inanna (Sumerian), Ishtar (Babylonian), Kali (Hindu), Kalma (Finnish), Kele-De (Irish), Lilith (Hebrew), Macha (Irish), Mara (Persian), Mari (Hindu), Mari-Ama (Norse), Marzana (Slavic), The Morrigan (Celtic), Nicnevin (Scottish), Pomona (Roman), Psyche (Greek), The Queen of Elphame (Scottish), Remati (Tibetan), Rhiannon (Welsh), and Zorya Vechernaya (Slavic).

Wizardry and Enchantments

Halloween is not only a night for contacting spirits, divination, and revelry. For Witches throughout the world it is also a time for conjuring, spellcasting, and brewing up the finest of potions.

Magick that inspires love, connects a Witch with the spirit world, or works like a magnet to attract good luck is traditionally practiced at this time of year. Since ancient times, there have existed three basic types of magick that Witches and other practitioners of the magickal arts have utilized. They are known as Imitative, Contagious, and Sympathetic.

Imitative magick dates back to prehistoric Europe, and is based on the primitive belief that the act of painting or drawing a picture of something happening will actually cause it to manifest. It is believed that many of the pictures painted on the walls of caves over twenty thousand years ago were created for magickal purposes. For instance, a painting of a hunter spearing his four-legged game would have served to magickally empower the hunter whom the painting depicted.

Contagious magick uses various items belonging to the person whom the spell is directed at. Such items commonly include, but are in no way limited to, an article of worn clothing, a lock of hair, and fingernail clippings. Historically, contagious magick has been used in both the arts of love enchantment and the casting of hexes on enemies.

Sympathetic magick, also known as *Image magick,* is a popular form of magick that operates on the basic principle that "like attracts like." It is common among those who practice Voodoo, African tribal magick, and Hoodoo folk magick. The sticking of pins into a Voodoo doll to bring pain or death to the person whom the doll represents is one example of the darker side of Sympathetic magick. Although the use of Voodoo dolls is generally uncommon

An engraving from the Douce Collection.

among practitioners of the Craft, many modern Witches have been known to employ special herb-stuffed cloth dolls known as "poppets" in their healing rituals and amatory enchantments. However, sorcery (also known as Black Magick) and the spreading of negative energy to harm others, gain revenge, or satisfy selfish desires is not what Halloween is about.

The majority of modern Witches adhere to a simple and benevolent moral code known as the Rede (or Wiccan Rede), which is as follows: "An' it harm none, do what thou wilt." The exact origin of the Rede is somewhat of a mystery, however, some writers have suggested that it is the Witches' version of the Christian's "Golden Rule." Its meaning is basically: Be free to do, either magickally or mundanely, what your heart tells you is the correct thing to do as long as your actions bring harm to none. Most Witches believe that if they work any form of magick that is contradictory to the Rede, bad karma (threefold or greater) will return to haunt him or her sooner or later.

HALLOWEEN CANDLE MAGICK

In olden times when Halloween night drew nigh and the season of the Witch made its presence strongly felt, many people throughout Europe burned special candles in their windows to light the way for, and welcome back, the returning spirits of deceased ancestors. Halloween candles were also employed as amulets to scare away any unfriendly ghosts that might be wandering about in the night in search of dwellings to haunt.

In the present day, the Halloween custom of candle

burning lives on in many parts of the world, including the United States. Candles molded into the shapes of Witches, grinning pumpkins, ghosts, skeletons, skulls, black cats, bats, owls, and other Halloween symbols can be found in most stores and are bought by the average person as nothing more than a holiday decoration. However, there is far more to Halloween candles than just their decorative function.

Candles that are fashioned in the stereotypical image of a Witch (with black cloak and pointed hat) are displayed on the shelves of many stores around Halloween time. Some are cute and whimsical, while others are intended to look wicked and haglike.

Some modern Witches are greatly insulted by such an irreverent and unflattering depiction of Witches. They feel it portrays them in an unfavorable fashion, is degrading to those in the Craft, and is greatly detrimental to the progress that many Witches' liberation activists have achieved in combatting the numerous negative stereotypes and misconceptions that have long been associated with Witches.

On the other hand, many Witches take little or no offense to the pointed hat-wearing Witch symbol. Instead, they find it to be humorous or charming. Some Witches even embrace it proudly as a kind of mascot, pointing out that the cone-shaped Witches' hat is an obvious phallic symbol which identifies Witchcraft's ancient roots as a European fertility religion. The hat is also a symbol of what is known as the cone of power (the raising of magickal energy). Either way, the image of a Witch is a highly powerful symbol and one that is extremely magickal.

Use white Witch-shaped candles in spells and rituals

that involve healing, divination, wisdom (Witchcraft is not called the "Craft of the Wise" for nothing), transformation, and the strengthening of clairvoyant or magickal abilities. They are also ideal as altar candles for initiation and self-dedication rites, as well as for meditational work. Black Witch-shaped candles work especially well in uncrossing rituals and banishing negativity.

Jack-o'-lanterns or pumpkin-shaped candles are appropriate for use in spells and rituals designed for protection against malevolent supernatural forces, negativity, enemies, destructive energies, and all manners of evil.

The image of a pumpkin naturally invokes the special magick of the autumn season, and in many circles it is a symbol of transition. Pumpkin candles are generally orange—a color which, in the art and practice of candle magick, increases the powers of concentration and feelings of courage.

Use any of the following anointment oils to increase a jack-o'-lantern or pumpkin-shaped candle's protective powers: cypress (ruled by the planet Saturn and the element of Earth), frankincense (ruled by the Sun and the element of Fire), geranium (ruled by the planet Venus and the element of Water), hazelnut (ruled by the Sun and the element of Air), myrrh (ruled by the Moon and the element of Water), olive (ruled by the Sun and the element of Fire), patchouli (ruled by the planet Saturn and the element of Earth), rosemary (ruled by the Sun and the element of Fire), or vervain (ruled by the planet Venus and the element of Earth).

Ghost-, skeleton-, and skull-shaped candles, with their obvious theme of death, are used by many Witches on Halloween in rituals designed to bless and/or welcome back the spirits of the dead. They are also used in seances and spirit channelings, and some people use them to illuminate their Ouija boards as they attempt to communicate with the world beyond.

Many modern-day necromancers (persons who practice the ancient occult method of divining the future through communication with the spirits of men, women, or children who have passed over to the other side) often use skull-shaped candles in their rituals to call forth the dead. In earlier times, candles affixed to the top of actual human skulls were utilized for this purpose.

The skull was, at one time, said to be the "seat of the soul." It was believed by many to possess potent magickal qualities, and it was viewed by most practitioners of the magickal arts as a focus of supernatural power. Its image in candle form is by no means deficient of magickal strength.

The essential oil of anise (ruled by the planet Jupiter and the element of Air) is traditionally used for anointing candles used in spells and rituals to conjure spirits. Orris oil (ruled by the planet Venus and the element of Water) has long been reputed to offer protection against evil spirits, while occult folklore holds that lavender oil (ruled by the planet Mercury and the element of Air), when it is used in the correct magickal manner, can bestow upon a human being the rare power to see ghosts.

Many Witches, especially those who are cat-lovers or who have a cat-familiar, use candles in the shape of black cats in spells designed to end streaks of bad luck, strengthen one's night vision, awaken or increase the powers of clairvoyance, restore balance, banish negative energies, and break the power of curses and hexes. Additionally, black cat candles are appropriate as altar candles for rituals that invoke and/or pay homage to the ancient Egyptian cat goddess Bastet.

Another popular candle found around Halloween is the bat. This mysterious creature of the night has been linked with Witchcraft and the darker side of superstition since the earliest of times. In the Middle Ages it was said that Witches used bats' blood as an ingredient in flying ointments, love potions, and spells to gain the power to see in the dark. It was also believed that Witches possessed the ability to shapeshift into bats by means of special charms and incantations. In bat form they could easily gain entry into people's houses, cause untold mischief, and then disappear quickly and unscathed into the darkness of the night.

Most Witches have always considered the bat to be a creature of good luck, even though it is regarded as an unlucky omen in a vast number of folkloric beliefs. Candles that resemble bats are highly effective tools of magick when used in spells and rituals designed to conjure forth good fortune, banish feelings of depression, strengthen one's night vision, and promote longevity.

A candle in the shape of an owl—another popular symbol of Halloween—is perfect for spells and rituals that are performed to gain wisdom. To make it an even more potent tool of magick, anoint the candle with seven drops of olive oil (ruled by the Sun and the element of Fire, and sacred to the goddess Athena) or sunflower oil (also ruled by the Sun and the element of Fire). **Note:** Seven is a significant number, in the ancient art and practice of numerology. It represents wisdom and knowledge, along with the mystery of time, secrets, and all things of a psychic or occult nature.

The number seven is also said to be more mystical and magickal than any other number.

A WITCH'S LUCKY CANDLE SPELL

To bring good luck into your life, take a brand new orange-colored candle that has never been lit and anoint it with three drops of cinnamon, clove, or lotus oil. (Each one of these oils is said to possess strong luck-attracting vibrations, which make them ideal for this spell.) When the clock strikes midnight on Halloween, light the candle with a match and thrice recite the following incantation:

> *Brimstone, moon, and Witch's fire,*
> *Candlelight's bright spell,*
> *Good luck shall I now acquire,*
> *Work thy magick well.*
> *Midnight twelve, the Witching Hour,*
> *Bring the luck I seek.*
> *By wax and wick now work thy power*
> *As these words I speak.*
> *Harming none, this spell is done.*
> *By law of three, so mote it be!*

Gaze into the flame of the candle and fill your mind only with thoughts about good luck. Visualize the Wheel of Fortune turning in your favor. Allow yourself to genuinely feel lucky, as though you had just won a prize. The more emotion you put into your spellcasting, the better the outcome will be. It is also important to never doubt the power of a spell, otherwise your negative thoughts will inadvertently undermine its effectiveness.

Allow the candle to burn until sunrise (the morning of November 1) and the spell shall be fixed. **Note:** To prevent accidental fires from occurring, many Witches place their candles in a sink or bathtub if they are to burn all night long unattended.

If the candle has not burned itself out, you may now extinguish its flame by pinching it out with your moistened fingertips or by using a candle snuffer. Remember, never blow out the flame with your breath because, according to old occult folklore, you will cause all of your good luck to blow away.

To peer into the future or into the realms of the unknown, sit before a mirror at midnight on Halloween. Place a black candle to the left of the mirror, and an orange candle to the right. With a match in each hand, light both candles at the same time, gaze into the reflection of your own eyes in the mirror and concentrate upon that which you desire to know until a vision (often misty at first) appears in the glass. Within this vision your answer may be found.

Another Halloween method of candle divination calls for a small cauldron to be filled with water in which a handful of mugwort gathered on Saint John's Eve (June 23) has been steeped. (Mugwort is an herb that has long been used by Witches to aid divination.) Light two pillar candles—one black and one orange—and hold them about one foot above the cauldron in your left and right hands, respectively. Concentrate upon whatever it is that you desire to know, and then recite it thirteen times in the form of a question as you tilt the candles so that the melted wax spills into the water below. Examine the patterns created by the black and orange wax to find a symbolic divinatory message.

A LOVER'S CANDLE SPELL

The following is an old Witches' love spell from England. It is traditionally performed on Halloween night and calls for the following items: a new candle (preferably pink in color), as many pins as you have suitors, and a strand of hair from each man's head (assuming that none of them are bald).

Begin by tying a strand of hair from one suitor to the first pin, a strand of hair from the next suitor to the second pin, and so forth. Stick the pins into the side of the candle, spacing them lengthwise. As each pin is stuck into the wax, recite the following magickal rhyme:

> *'Tis not this candle alone I stick,*
> *But my love's heart I mean to prick.*

Light the candle with a match and watch it as it burns down to the first pin, and then to the next. When it reaches the pin of your true mate, the front door is supposed to open and your true love will appear.

THE PUMPKIN-OF-PASSION LOVE SPELL

To bring two people together in a romantic fashion, perform this amatory enchantment during the Venus hour on Halloween. Ancient occult tradition holds that the hours ruled by the planet Venus and under the influence of the Roman love goddess after whom this planet is named, are the ideal hours for casting love spells. They are also believed to be the appropriate times for brewing love potions (known as "philtres" in ancient times), performing love divinations, and basically engaging in any form of magick relating to matters of the heart.

According to the ancient grimoire (textbook of magick) known as *The Key of Solomon*, the planetary hours of Venus for each day of the week are as follows:

Sunday: 2 A.M., 9 A.M., 4 P.M., 11 P.M.
Monday: 6 A.M., 1 P.M., 8 P.M.
Tuesday: 3 A.M., 10 A.M., 5 P.M., midnight
Wednesday: 7 A.M., 2 P.M., 9 P.M.
Thursday: 4 A.M., 11 A.M., 6 P.M.
Friday: 1 A.M., 8 A.M., 3 P.M., 10 P.M.
Saturday: 5 A.M., noon, 7 P.M.

Using a consecrated athame, cut a lid in the top of a small pumpkin. Remove the lid, clean out the pumpkin, and then place inside of it the following magickal ingredients: a heart-shaped piece of red wax upon which the names (written in runes) and astrological symbols of the two intended lovers have been inscribed, a lock of hair from each person at whom this spell is directed, a handful of red or pink rose petals (a plant associated with love magick), a seashell (a symbol sacred to the love goddess Aphrodite), and a pinch of powdered orris root (a most powerful ingredient of love spells). Replace the lid on the top of the pumpkin, and enchant it by thrice reciting the following incantation over it:

Earth below and moon above,
Bring to life this charm of love.
With thy secret powers true
Let the pangs of love ensue.
Moon above and Earth below,
I pray thee yearning to bestow
Upon the two who share one heart:
Let now the enchantment start.
So mote it be!

Wrap the pumpkin in a piece of red satin and secretly bury it in the ground beneath the rays of the moon. The pumpkin-of-passion love spell is now complete.

To reverse this spell, carefully dig up the heart-shaped piece of red wax and destroy it by casting it into a fire or into a pot of boiling water as you recite the original incantation backwards. Be sure to do this on a night when the moon is in a waning phase, for this is the appropriate time to reverse love spells and perform magick that brings things to an end.

If done correctly, the magickally inspired feelings of love between the two people whose names were inscribed upon the wax will immediately begin to subside.

HALLOWEEN LEAF MAGICK

It is said that on Halloween there is great magick to be found in an autumn leaf falling from a tree, but only if the leaf is caught by human hands before it makes its landing. Once a leaf has touched the ground, its magick is forever lost, according to folklore.

The Halloween tradition of catching a falling leaf originated long ago in England, where it was believed to ensure
continued happiness for the next twelve months or else
make a special wish come true. Another variation of this
tradition runs that a falling leaf caught before reaching the
ground on Halloween will ensure good health throughout
the winter season.

A simple Witch's spell is said to guarantee one day
of happiness for each falling leaf that is caught between
Michaelmas (the annual feast of the archangel Michael, observed on September 29) and Halloween. However, take care
not to bring any dead leaves into your house! Those who subscribe to superstitious thought claim that unless dead leaves
blow into your house on their own accord, they will render
your home and family extremely vulnerable to bad luck.

THE SECRET WISH MIRROR SPELL

This simple, yet potent, spell dates back to antiquity and is a
Halloween tradition among many Witches. To perform this
spell you will need three things: an ordinary mirror, a candle that has never been lit before, and a sincere wish.

Begin after sunset on Halloween night by lighting the
candle with a match. (If you desire, you may anoint the candle with three drops of your favorite ritual oil prior to working this spell.) Turn off all the lights in the room and stand
before the mirror, holding the lit candle in your power
hand. Gaze into the reflection of your own eyes and clear
your mind of all thoughts, except for those pertaining to
your wish. Visualize your wish coming true as you whisper
the following incantation:

Looking glass and Witch's flame
Let thy powers interweave
Grant the wish that I proclaim
On this most enchanted eve.
My secret wish is . . . (state your wish)
So mote it be!

Gently place your lips upon the mirror to seal the spell with a kiss. The secret wish mirror spell is now complete, but take care not to reveal your secret wish to anybody or else it will not manifest.

Witches have utilized mirrors for spellcasting and divination since antiquity.

A HALLOWEEN SPELL TO
DESTROY WEAKNESS

For many Witches who celebrate the Sabbat of Samhain/
Halloween, the last day of October is an ideal time for magickally doing away with any type of weakness, just as for the
Celts of old it was the time to slaughter all livestock that
were too weak to live through the coming winter.

One modern Halloween spell to destroy weakness calls
for the following items: a piece of parchment paper,
dragon's blood ink (available in most occult shops and mail
order catalogues), and a Samhain bonfire. (If an outdoor
fire is not possible, do not despair. A black candle and any
fireproof container, such as an ashtray or a cast iron cauldron, can be used to take its place.)

Using the dragon's blood ink, write on the piece of
parchment whatever weakness or weaknesses you wish to be
rid of. Crumple up the paper as you concentrate upon your
intent, and then either toss it into the bonfire or set it ablaze
by holding it above the flame of the black candle and then
place it into the fireproof container. As the parchment burns
to ashes, so, too, will your weaknesses be destroyed by the
flames of magick.

A BLOOD SPELL TO PROTECT A HOUSE

A very old spell that hails from Ireland calls for the fresh
blood of a young rooster to be sprinkled at the corners of a
house to keep it safe from the hauntings of ghosts and the
spells and curses of sorcerers.

Although this spell has long been associated with Martinmas, there is little doubt that it was at one time a Samhain practice, since the date on which Martinmas is currently celebrated, November 11, is actually November 1 (Samhain) according to the old Julian calendar.

ROWAN TREE PROTECTION SPELL

To keep yourself safe on Halloween from bewitchment, ill wishes, or the evil doings of supernatural beings, cut a branch of the rowan tree that is covered with red berries. With a red thread, attach it to your clothing or hair as you thrice recite the following magickal verse:

> *Rowan tree and red thread*
> *Gar the Witches dance their dead.*

The rowan tree has long been regarded as the most magickal of all trees, and its protective powers are legendary. However, if you are unable to find a rowan tree to complete this spell, you can still protect yourself on Halloween simply by wearing something that is red. According to occult folklore, the color red works exceptionally well in keeping sorcerers and supernaturals at bay.

GARLIC SPELL

To keep evil spirits at bay, people in Scotland once hung garlic around their houses on Halloween.

Believed to also ward off vampires, wicked Witches, demons, and all persons possessing the evil eye, the use of garlic for protection against the supernatural is common in many cultures and dates back to the most ancient of times.

A CHARM AGAINST DRUNKENNESS

It was once believed that a forked twig cut from a hazel tree at the witching hour on Halloween and carried in a pocket or mojo bag worked as a powerful magickal charm to prevent intoxication, regardless of how much alcohol was consumed. Hazel twigs have also been used for attracting good luck, making wishes come true, and protecting sailors from disasters at sea.

A MODERN WITCHES' SPELL TO BRING RECONCILIATION

In Druidic times, Samhain was a time to set right any matters that caused dissension between members of the tribe. In keeping with this old tradition, many modern Witches and Pagans perform a spell on Halloween night, if necessary, to reconcile differences and heal anger between friends or lovers.

To perform such a spell you will need a piece of parchment, dove's blood ink (available in most occult shops and mail order catalogues), and a hallowed fire source such as a Sabbat bonfire, a sacred cauldron fire, or even a candle burning within a jack-o'-lantern.

Begin by writing, in dove's blood ink, your intent upon the piece of parchment. After thrice reciting the following incantation, close your eyes and visualize your intent as being manifest, and then cast the parchment into the bonfire or blazing cauldron, or light it by holding it over the flame of the jack-o'-lantern's candle and then place it in a fireproof container and allow it to burn away to ashes:

> *Nicnevin, Nicnevin,*
> *O ancient Crone of wisdom,*
> *upon thee I call*
> *on this darkest of nights.*
> *Nicnevin, Nicnevin,*
> *O governess of magick,*
> *with love I beseech thee*
> *empower this rite.*
> *My spell I do fashion*
> *and cast it with passion*
> *by Witches' law of three:*
> *As I will, so mote it be!*

GEMSTONE MAGICK

To ensure prosperity in the coming year, according to ancient occult tradition, wear or carry within a charm bag, a piece of black agate. For this charm to work, you must do this from midnight of Halloween eve until midnight of Halloween night.

Rub a piece of black jade nine times on Halloween in order to gain strength and power. Jade is a stone possessing intense occult vibrations, and its magickal employment has been a part of Oriental culture since ancient times.

To prevent nightmares and unpleasant dreams from

plaguing you, and to keep yourself protected against incubus or succubus demons while you sleep, place an onyx stone beneath your pillow before you retire to bed on Halloween night.

A WITCH'S NEW YEAR CHANT

The following chant is designed for coven use; however, it can be easily adapted for solitaries simply by changing the words "we" and "our" to "I" and "my", respectively.

On the 31st of October (the eve of the Witches' New Year), join hands to form a circle around a glowing jack-o'-lantern. Concentrate upon your New Year's resolutions while repeating the following chant over and over, each time a bit louder and stronger until sufficient magickal energy has been raised and you feel your body tingling:

> *Samhain Eve,*
> *We chant, we weave*
> *A web of magick for to cleave.*
> *Spells conceive,*
> *In love believe,*
> *Our new year's goals*
> *We shall achieve!*

Gradually lower the chant, and then end it with:

> *So mote it be!*

Don't forget to uncast the circle.

Halloween night is the traditional time for performing all manners of divination. One method commonly employed by modern Witches is the reading of Tarot cards, which offer guidance as well as reveal situations and influences from the past, present, and future.

The Tarot can also be used for meditation purposes. This is done by selecting a certain card from the deck, holding it in your power hand, and contemplating its meaning. Tarot meditations can be enhanced by the burning of candles and incense, and any card from either the Major or Minor Arcana can be utilized.

For Halloween meditations with the Tarot, the appropriate card to use is the Death card, as the themes of death and transformation are strongly connected to Halloween through its historical background and symbolism.

According to cartomancers (persons who read fortune telling cards), the card of Death rarely ever signifies an actual physical death when it appears in a person's reading. In most cases, it is a card that speaks of transformation and unexpected changes: the "death" of the old and the "birth" of the new, alteration, endings and renewals, and so forth. In this sense it is often viewed as a positive card. But this is not to say that this card can never mean an actual death or the loss of something such as a job or financial security. However, before such an interpretation can be established, such things as the card's position in the layout and the meanings of the surrounding cards must be taken into careful consideration.

The card of Death is the perfect meditation card to use

DEATH.

when you are ready to release the past and accept the ending of something in order for positive changes and new beginnings to come. In addition, it can offer emotional healing to those who mourn the death of a beloved family member or friend.

A FAIRY SPELL

A spell to enable a person to perceive fairy rings and to hear the sound of fairy music calls for the following herbs to be gathered, diced, and then baked into a tiny oaten cake: bay, mistletoe, rue, thyme, vervain, and yarrow. Anoint the cake with a bit of honey and three drops of rose oil.

On Halloween night, as the moon of enchantment is rising in the sky above, place the sweetened cake under a tree or a bush in your garden as an offering to the fairy folk. According to Witches' lore, if your magick is true and your heart filled only with sincerity, the fairies will open their secret and wondrous world to you right before your very eyes.

The other times of the year when such a spell is said to be effective are: at moonrise on Lady Day (March 25), Easter, the first day of May (known as May Day, Beltane, and Walpurgis), the Summer Solstice (June 21), Christmas Eve, and Christmas Day.

A HALLOWEEN CHARM

The following spoken charm may be recited prior to the performing of any Halloween divination involving fire-gazing or the scrying of magick-mirrors.

Let the sacred fires burn bright.
Let the spirits rise and the moon make her magick.
Behold the shadows as they dance, while the cold wind
whispers its ancient incantations.
Cast the circle and read the signs.
Magick is afoot in the witching hour.
Let the love of the Old Ones light the way.
May the wisdom of the ages through candle-glow and
magick-mirror be revealed.
And as it is willed, so mote it be!

TO BLESS THE DEAD

On Halloween night, anoint a black candle with three drops of frankincense or myrrh oil (or a blend of the two) to consecrate it. Light the candle's wick with a match, and say:

Flame of magick, come to life.
In thy power be most rife!

Fill your mind with images of your deceased loved one. Take a black feather in your power hand and use it to trace the symbol of the pentagram in the air over the flame of the candle. Do this thrice, each time reciting the following incantation:

> *Blessed be my* (state relationship) *deceased,*
> *From earthly chains be now released,*
> *Pain and sorrow be now ceased,*
> *May thy spirit rest in peace.*
> *As it is willed, so mote it be.*

A Traditional
Halloween Cookery

Food has long played an important role in the celebration of Halloween. It has been used in various cultures for divinatory and amuletic purposes, as well as to symbolize, bless, and nourish the hungry souls of the dead.

In Druidic times, elaborate feasts were set out each year at Halloween. Magick was abound not only in the mesmerizing flames of the sacred bonfires and the dark shadows of the spirit-haunted night, but in the food and drink of the season as well.

In many parts of the world, there can be found old legends warning that food should never be left out overnight on Halloween because fairies will enchant it, the spirits of the dead will devour it, Witches and Warlocks will steal, poison, or curse it, or the Devil will leave his diabolical mark upon it, rendering it unsafe for any man, woman, child, or beast to consume!

Halloween is the traditional time for Pagan folks throughout the world to provide the inhabitants of both the fairy and spirit worlds with offerings of various foods. In the seventeenth-century book, *Remaines*, the custom of leaving offerings to the fairy folk is described in the following manner: "They were wont to please the Fairies, that they might doe them no shrewd turnes, by sweeping the Hearth and setting by it a dish of fair water halfe sadd. . . . bread, whereon was set a messe of milke sopt with white bread."

Halloween and its foods are no strangers to superstition. An old wive's tale that lingers on in modern times holds that it is extremely unlucky, even dangerous, for any person to bake bread after the sun has set on Halloween. To accidentally burn a loaf of bread on Halloween or throw bread crumbs or crusts into the fire brings ill luck and "feeds the Devil." A loaf of bread laid the wrong side up is said to invite the Devil into the house. Some superstitious Christians still believe that it is bad luck to forget saying grace before dining on Halloween.

THE DUMB SUPPER

A Halloween tradition once popular in Ireland and parts of Great Britain, the Dumb Supper was the ritual offering of food to the spirits of the dead who came to call on this night. In Ireland, it was not uncommon for tobacco, a dish of porridge, and empty chairs to be set out in front of the hearth in anticipation of visiting spirits. In Paul Huson's *Mastering Witchcraft*, he describes the Dumb Supper as an offering of wine and a cake-shaped loaf of bread "made in nine segments similar to the square of Earth."

SOUL CAKES

In the Middle Ages, bakeries throughout central and southern England were filled each year on All Souls' Day with little square buns decorated with currants and known as "soul cakes." These sweetened rolls were eaten to bring mercy on the souls of all Christians who had died within the past year.

Soul cakes were as important on All Souls' Day as hot cross buns were on Good Friday and plum pudding was on Christmas. They are believed to be a custom that derived from an old Pagan tradition of baking bread from the new grain at the Samhain harvest festival.

Soulers (people who would walk the streets on All Souls' Day singing and begging for food and money) would be given soul cakes in return saying additional prayers for the deceased loved ones of the donors. It was believed that the passage of the dead soul through purgatory was made faster by each prayer that was offered up.

In Yorkshire, England, the baking of special *saumas* (soul mass) loaves was a custom related to the soul cake. Bakers were known to give these small round loaves away to their favorite customers to bring them good luck. As a charm against early death, one or two loaves would be kept in each house until the next All Souls' Day.

On Halloween, children in Belgium used to stand beside little shrines erected in front of their homes and sell "Cakes for the Dead" (small white cakes or cookies). A cake was eaten for each spirit honored in the belief that the more cakes you consumed, the more blessings you would receive from the dead.

OTHER TRADITIONAL FOODS
OF HALLOWEEN

At Samhain, the Druid priests ritually slaughtered oxen for divinatory purposes, and the parts of the animals they didn't use were roasted in the purifying Samhain bonfire and then served to the tribe at the New Year's feast.

Hundreds of years later, ritual food known as "sowens" was eaten in Scotland and parts of Ireland on Halloween. The poet Robert Burns once said: "Sowens, with butter instead of milk to them, is always the Hallowe'en Supper." (Interestingly, but hardly coincidentally, the words "sowen" and "Samhain" are nearly identical in their pronunciations.) The definition of a sowen, according to the *Oxford English Dictionary*, is "an article of diet formerly in common use in Scotland (and in some parts of Ireland), consisting of farinaceous matter extracted from the bran or husks of oats by steeping in water, allowed to ferment slightly and prepared by boiling."

Apples, squash, and pork are listed as the corresponding foods of Samhain in Edain McCoy's *The Sabbats*. Among the herbs and spices traditional to Halloween are: allspice, catnip, mugwort, and sage.

Patricia Telesco's *Seasons of the Sun* lists the ritual foods of Halloween as: pumpkin or apple pie, and a harvest stew containing such ingredients as corn, zucchini, and chunks of turnips. Acorns, apples, corn stalks, gourds, hazelnuts (for protection), and squash are listed as "decorating ideas."

In Ireland, one traditional Halloween food was *barm brack*—a dark brown loaf or cake made with dried fruit and containing various tokens, such as rings, beans, peas, and so forth. Used for love divination, barm brack is traditionally cut and buttered by a married person and then served. The token found in one's slice delivers a divinatory message to that person. (For instance, a ring means that marriage will take place within the next twelve months; a pea means a life plagued by financial struggles; a bean promises a future filled with wealth; a rag indicates that its recipient will remain unmarried for at least another year; and so forth.) Barm brack is still baked in Ireland at Halloween time, and is even sold commercially.

Another traditional Halloween food of Ireland—especially popular in the northern counties of Cavan and Donegal—is a potato dish known as *boxty*. It is made with equal amounts of raw potatoes (grated and strained), cooked mashed potatoes, and flour. Salt, pepper, and melted butter or fat can also be added. The dough mixture is kneaded and formed into round flat cakes. A "cross" (X) is marked upon the top of each cake with the tip of a sharp knife and then they are baked in the oven. Sometimes baking soda and milk are added to the mixture to make it into a batter, which is then fried on a hot griddle to make boxty pancakes. They are sprinkled with sugar and buttered. Before eating boxty on Halloween, a single woman who desired herself a husband was required to thrice repeat the following rhyme:

> *Boxty on the griddle,*
> *boxty in the pan,*
> *If you don't eat boxty,*
> *you'll never get a man.*

Colcannon, a dish consisting of mashed potatoes, parsnips, and chopped onions, was another popular Irish food served at Halloween and used for divinatory purposes, especially where amatory interests were concerned. In Scotland, a similar dish known as *champit taties* was used by Halloween fortune tellers in a nearly identical fashion. (For more details, see the section "Halloween Food Divination" in the chapter: "Divinations and Incantations.")

Crowdie, a sweet apple cream dessert, was a traditional All Hallow's Eve food in many parts of the British Isles during the Middle Ages. Containing two coins, two wedding rings and two marbles, it would be shared among six people who desired to know what the future held in store for them. Wealth and success was indicated for those who got a coin; marriage for those who got a ring; and a life of loneliness for those unfortunate enough to get a marble. If nothing was found in one's portion of the divinatory dessert, it meant that his or her future would be full of uncertainty.

In the United States, candy and caramel apples are associated with Halloween by most people from coast to coast, as the custom here is for costumed children to go around the neighborhood, from house to house, shouting "Trick or treat!" and receiving handouts of assorted sweets.

In many rural regions of the United States, it was not uncommon to once find hollowed-out pumpkins filled with apples, raisins, nuts, and other harvest fruits decorating banquet tables at Halloween. Other foods popular among the country folk at this time of year included gingerbread, buttered popcorn, doughnuts, roasted pumpkin seeds, and just about anything made from fresh pumpkins, such as pies, cookies, and muffins. The traditional beverage of Halloween has always been, and most likely will always be, apple cider.

HALLOWEEN RECIPES

The following is a collection of traditional Halloween food recipes culled from various parts of the world. Slightly altered to conform to modern cooking methods, they are guaranteed to invoke the spirit of an old-fashioned Halloween.

MANDRAGORA (MANDRAKE) WINE

    13 apples
       Fruit of one May Apple (American
       Mandrake)
     7 lbs. sugar (16 cups)
     2 gallons water
     3 oranges
     3 lemons
     1 yeast cake (or 1 envelope dry yeast)

Remove the stems, skins, and seeds from the apples, and boil for approximately twenty minutes. Drain and mash together with the fully ripe, oval, lemon-colored fruit of one May Apple plant. **CAUTION:** Do not use any other part of the May Apple. Its fully ripe fruit is edible, but the rest of the plant is extremely toxic!

Add the sugar to the water. Slice the oranges and lemons, leaving the peels intact but removing the seeds. Add the oranges, lemons, apples, and May Apple fruit to the liquid. Boil for 20 minutes and then remove from heat. Let it stand for 24 hours.

In a separate bowl, dissolve yeast in 6 tablespoons of hot water. Add mixture to fruit. Stir and then strain the mixture through a wet muslin or cheesecloth into wine bottles, filling them to the brim. Tie pieces of muslin over the bottle tops or seal with corks. Do not cap the bottles too tightly. Small amounts of gas may form and must be allowed to escape.

The wine is ready to drink after fermentation has stopped and no more bubbles appear in the bottles. Store in a dark cool place (such as a wine cellar or basement) for up to six months. Yields about 9 bottles.

BREAD OF THE DEAD

2 envelopes yeast
½ cup lukewarm water
2 beaten eggs, divided
2 tablespoons melted lard (shortening or butter may be substituted)
2 tablespoons fresh orange zest
4 cups flour
1 cup sugar (granulated)
2 teaspoons salt
1 beaten egg

Dissolve the yeast in the lukewarm water. Stir in two beaten eggs, lard, and orange zest. In a separate bowl, sift together flour, sugar, and salt, and add to the yeast mixture, stirring in a clockwise direction. Turn the dough out onto a flour-covered board and knead with your hands for about 10 minutes. Place the dough in a large bowl or pot, cover, and allow it to rise for one hour.

Punch down the risen dough. Cut off one-third of the dough and set it aside. On a large, well-greased cookie sheet, form the remaining dough into the shape of a skull. With a sharp knife, carefully carve out eyes, nose, and mouth. Use the reserved dough to form crossbones.

Let the dough rise for another hour, and then bake for 30 minutes in a 350 degree oven. Remove from oven and use some of the last beaten egg to "glue" the crossbones to the skull. Brush the entire loaf with the rest of the egg, sprinkle with sugar, and then return it to the oven. Bake for an additional 10 to 20 minutes or until the color of the loaf is golden and it gives off a hollow sound when tapped. Set it on a wire rack to cool. (This recipe yields one loaf of bread.)

COLCANNON

             10 large potatoes (5 lbs.)
              1 head cabbage (or kale)
              1 onion (Scallions or chives may be substituted)
            1⅓ cups milk
              1 stick (½ cup) butter or margarine
              2 teaspoons salt
             ½ teaspoon ground black pepper

Wash and peel the potatoes. Remove the eyes, sprouts, or any green areas, and then cut into quarters. Put the potatoes in a large pot of boiling salted water.

Wash and chop up the head of cabbage and the onion. Put them into the pot with the potatoes. Cover, and cook for 25 minutes or until the potatoes are tender.

Drain in a strainer or colander, and return to the pot. Mash (or whip with an electric mixer until blended) and stir in the milk, butter or margarine, salt, and pepper. Serves 6.

SAMHAIN CIDER

2 quarts apple cider
½ cup confectioner's sugar
½ teaspoon nutmeg
½ teaspoon cinnamon
¼ teaspoon ginger
½ cup apricot brandy

In a large pot, combine the apple cider, confectioner's sugar, nutmeg, cinnamon, and ginger. Simmer slowly on low heat for about 15 minutes. Take care that the cider does not boil. Add the apricot brandy and then serve the cider while it is still warm. Refrigerate any leftover cider. Serves 8.

OLD-FASHIONED MULLED CIDER

3 quarts (12 cups) apple cider
4 whole cloves
3 cinnamon sticks
1 cup dark rum

In a large pot, combine the apple cider, cloves, and cinnamon sticks. Bring to a boil over medium-high heat. Reduce the heat and allow the cider to simmer uncovered for 25 to 35 minutes.

Pour the cider mixture through a cheesecloth-lined strainer into a large saucepan, and keep warm. When ready to serve, put 1 or 2 tablespoons of dark rum into each mug, and then fill to the rim with the mulled cider. If desired, garnish with orange slices, whole cloves, and cinnamon sticks. Serves 12.

HAZELNUT COOKIES

1¾ cups flour
1 teaspoon baking powder
½ teaspoon baking soda
½ teaspoon salt
1 teaspoon nutmeg
1 teaspoon cinnamon
¼ pound butter or margarine
1 teaspoon vanilla
1 cup sugar
2 eggs
1½ cups chopped hazelnuts
1 cup raisins

Sift together the flour, baking powder, baking soda, salt, nutmeg, and cinnamon. Set aside. In a large bowl, cream the butter. Add the vanilla and sugar and beat well. Add the eggs and beat until the mixture is smooth. Gradually add the sifted dry ingredients, beating until thoroughly mixed. Stir in the hazelnuts and raisins.

Preheat oven to 400 degrees. Place well rounded teaspoonsful of the dough about two inches apart on a foil-covered cookie sheet. Bake for 12 to 15 minutes. Yields about 2 dozen cookies.

CORN PUDDING

3 cups milk
8 egg whites
4¾ cups cooked corn kernels
⅓ minced onion
1 teaspoon salt

In a large saucepan, heat the milk until just before it reaches the boiling point. Remove from heat. Blend the egg whites and two cups of the corn in a blender or food processor until almost smooth. Add the remaining corn, onion, and salt, and then stir in the egg mixture.

Preheat oven to 325 degrees. Pour into a well greased two-quart baking dish. Bake for 45 minutes, or until the corn pudding feels firm to the touch. Serves 12.

SQUASH AND CHEDDAR PIE

1 tablespoon butter or margarine
1 cup chopped onion
3 eggs
3 cups winter squash, cooked and mashed
½ cup milk
1 cup shredded cheddar cheese
1 teaspoon salt
2 tablespoons chopped fresh dill
½ teaspoon ground black pepper

In a medium-size skillet, melt the butter over medium heat. Add the chopped onion and cook for about ten minutes, stirring occasionally, until the onion is tender and golden in color.

In a large bowl, beat the eggs with a fork or a wire wisk. Stir in the squash, milk, ½ cup of cheddar cheese, salt, dill, and pepper. Add the onion mixture.

Preheat oven to 350 degrees. Ladle into lightly greased custard cups and place on a baking sheet. Sprinkle the tops with the remaining ½ cup of cheese. Bake for approximately thirty minutes, or until a toothpick inserted in the centers comes out clean. Place the custard cups on a wire rack to cool for five minutes, and then serve. Serves 7.

PUMPKIN MUFFINS

2 cups flour
2 teaspoons baking powder
1 teaspoon baking soda
½ teaspoon salt
1 stick butter or margarine, softened
½ cup sugar
2 eggs
½ cup buttermilk
⅔ cup cooked, mashed pumpkin (canned pumpkin can be used)
¼ cup brown sugar
2 tablespoons molasses (dark)
½ teaspoon cinnamon
½ teaspoon ginger
½ teaspoon ground cloves (or allspice)

In a small bowl, sift together the flour, baking powder, baking soda, and salt. In a separate large bowl, beat the butter and sugar until they are fluffy in texture and pale in color. Beat in the eggs and buttermilk until well blended. Add the flour mixture to form a batter.

Preheat oven to 375 degrees. In a medium-size bowl, mix together the pumpkin, brown sugar, molasses, cinnamon, ginger, and ground cloves until well blended. Stir into the batter.

Ladle the batter into twelve 2½-inch greased muffin cups and bake for 15 to 17 minutes, or until a toothpick inserted into the center of a muffin comes out clean. Cool on a wire rack for five minutes, and then turn the muffins out onto the rack and allow them to cool completely. Yields 12 muffins.

SEASON OF THE CRONE

Crone of Winter's spellbound cold,
in Her cauldron of black are told
secrets ancient, truths and tales:
mystery Her light unveils.

She is wisdom, She is changes:
time and space She rearranges.
In Her hands, the card of Death,
for transformation is Her breath.

Crone of Winter, Grandmother wise,
look into Her gargoyle eyes.
Let Her lessons teach you well:
life is but a magick spell.

—from *Priestess and Pentacle*
by Gerina Dunwich

BIBLIOGRAPHY

Bannatyne, Lesley Pratt. *Halloween: An American Holiday, an American History*. New York: Facts on File, 1990.

Barth, Edna. *Witches, Pumpkins, and Grinning Ghosts*. New York: Clarion Books, 1972.

Bonwick, J. *Irish Druids and Irish Religions*. Marlboro, England: Dorset Press, 1986. (originally published in 1894 by Griffin Farran and Co., London.)

Bord, Janet and Colin. *Dictionary of Earth Mysteries*. London: Thorsons, 1996.

Burland, C. A. *Echoes of Magic*. London: Peter Davies, 1972.

Camden, William. *Remaines, Concerning Britain*. London: Symon Waterson, 1629.

Campanelli, Pauline. *Wheel of the Year: Living the Magical Life*. St. Paul, MN: Llewellyn Publications, 1995.

Corkery, Daniel. *The Hidden Ireland*. Dublin, Ireland: Gill and Macmillan, 1967.

Crawford, Saffi and Geraldine Sullivan. *The Power of Birthdays, Stars, and Numbers*. New York: The Ballantine Publishing Group, 1998.

Cunliffe, Barry. *The Ancient Celts*. New York: Oxford University Press, 1967.

Cunningham, Scott. *Living Wicca*. St. Paul, MN: Llewellyn Publications, 1993.

Curtin, Jeremiah. *Myths and Folk Tales of Ireland*. New York: Dover Books, 1975.

Davidson, H. E. *Myths and Symbols in Pagan Europe*. Manchester, England: Manchester University Press, 1988.

Ellis, Peter Berresford. *A Dictionary of Irish Mythology*. London: Constable and Company Limited, 1987.

———. *The Druids*. London: Constable and Company Limited, 1994.

Evans-Wentz, W. Y. *The Fairy Faith in Celtic Countries*. New York: Lemma Publishing Company, 1973.

Farrar, Janet and Stewart. *Eight Sabbats for Witches*. Custer, Washington: Phoenix Publishing, 1981.

Ferguson, Diana. *The Magickal Year*. York Beach, Maine: Samuel Weiser, Inc., 1996.

Folklore, Myths and Legends of Britain. London: Reader's Digest, 1973.

Graves, Robert. *The White Goddess*. New York: Vintage Books, 1958.

Green, Miranda. *Dictionary of Celtic Myth and Lore*. London: Thames and Hudson, 1992.

———. *Celtic Goddesses: Warriors, Virgins, and Mothers*. London: British Museum Press, 1995.

Guiley, Rosemary Ellen. *The Encyclopedia of Witches and Witchcraft*. New York: Facts on File, 1989.

———. *The Encyclopedia of Ghosts and Spirits*. New York: Facts on File, 1992.

Harbison, Peter. *Pre-Christian Ireland*. London: Thames and Hudson, 1988.

Hazlitt, W. Carew. *Faith and Folklore of the British Isles*. London: Reeves and Turner, 1905.

Huson, Paul. *Mastering Witchcraft*. New York: G.P. Putnam's Sons, 1970.

Hutton, Ronald. *The Pagan Religions of the Ancient British Isles.* Oxford, England: Blackwell, 1993.

Jones, Prudence and Nigel Pennick. *A History of Pagan Europe.* London: Routledge, 1995.

Jones, T. G. *Welsh Folk-Lore and Folk-Custom.* London: Methuen, 1930.

Jordan, Michael. *Encyclopedia of Gods: Over 2,500 Deities of the World.* New York: Facts on File, 1993.

Kendrick, T. D. *The Druids.* London: Frank Cass, 1966.

King James I. *Daemonologie.* Booklet, reprint of 1597 edition, publisher unknown.

Leach, Maria, ed. *Dictionary of Folklore, Mythology, and Legend.* London: New English Library, 1972.

Linton, Ralph and Adelin Linton. *Halloween Through Twenty Centuries.* New York: Henry Schuman, 1950.

McCoy, Edain. *The Sabbats.* St. Paul, MN: Llewellyn Publications, 1996.

————. *A Witch's Guide to Faery Folk.* St. Paul, MN: Llewellyn Publications, 1997.

Mackenzie, D. A. *Scottish Folk-Lore and Folk Life.* London: Blackie and Son, 1935.

MacManus, Diarmiud. *Irish Earth Folk.* New York: Devin-Adair Company, 1959.

Martin, M. *Description of the Western Islands of Scotland.* Edinburgh: James Thin, 1970 (modern reprint of Second Edition, originally published 1716).

McNeill, F. Marian. *Halloween: Its Origins, Rites and Ceremonies in the Scottish Tradition.* Edinburgh, Ireland: The Albyn Press, 1970.

Matthews, Caitlin and John Matthews. *The Encyclopaedia of Celtic Wisdom.* Rockport, Maine: Element Books, Inc., 1994.

O'Hogain, Dr. Daithi. *Myth, Legend, and Romance: An Encyclopedia of the Irish Folk Tradition.* London: Ryan Publishing, 1990.

O'Rahilly, T. F. *Early Irish History and Mythology*. Dublin, Ireland: Dublin Institute for Advanced Studies, 1976.

Odor, Ruth Shannon. *Halloween Handbook*. Chicago: Children's Press, 1984.

Opie, Iona and Moira Tatem. *A Dictionary of Superstitions*. New York: Oxford University Press, 1989.

Parry-Jones, D. *Welsh Legends and Fairy Lore*. London: Batsford, 1953.

Pickering, David. *Dictionary of Superstitions*. London: Cassell, 1995.

RavenWolf, Silver. "The Origins of Halloween," *Llewellyn's Witches' Datebook*. St. Paul, MN: Llewellyn Publications, 1999.

Rees, Alwyn and Brinley Rees. *Celtic Heritage*. London: Thames and Hudson, 1961.

Robbins, Rossell Hope. *The Encyclopedia of Witchcraft and Demonology*. New York: Bonanza Books, 1959.

Ross, Anne. *Pagan Celtic Britain*. London: Cardinal, 1974.

Russell, Jeffrey B. *History of Witchcraft*. New York: Thames and Hudson, 1980.

Simpson, Jacqueline. *The Folklore of the Welsh Border*. London: Batsford, 1976.

Sinclair, George. *Satan's Invisible World Discovered*. Edinburgh: T. MacCleish and Company, 1808.

Solomon. *The Key of Solomon the King*. York Beach, ME: Samuel Weiser, 1989. (Translated and edited from the original manuscript in the British Museum by S. Liddell MacGregor.)

Spence, Lewis. *Magic Arts in Celtic Britain*. London: Aquarian Press, 1970.

Stewart MacAlister, R. A. (ed.). *Lebor Gabala Erann (The Book of the Taking of Ireland)*. Dublin: Irish Texts Society, 1958.

Strange Stories, Amazing Facts. Pleasantville, NY: The Reader's Digest Association, Inc., 1976.

Telesco, Patricia. *Seasons of the Sun*. York Beach, ME: Samuel Weiser, 1996.

Trevelyan, M. *Folk-Lore and Folk-Stories of Wales*. London: Eliot Stock, 1909.

Van Hamel, A. G. *Aspects of Celtic Mythology*. London: British Academy Press, 1935.

Van Straalen, Alice. *The Book of Holidays Around the World*. New York: E. P. Dutton, 1986.

Walker, Barbara G. *The Women's Book of Myths and Secrets*. Edison, NJ: Castle Books, 1996.

Waring, Philippa. *A Dictionary of Omens and Superstitions*. London: Souvenir Press, 1978.

INDEX

FOR THE BEST IN PAPERBACKS, LOOK FOR THE

In every corner of the world, on every subject under the sun, Penguin represents quality and variety—the very best in publishing today.

For complete information about books available from Penguin—including Puffins, Penguin Classics, and Arkana—and how to order them, write to us at the appropriate address below. Please note that for copyright reasons the selection of books varies from country to country.

In the United Kingdom: Please write to *Dept. EP, Penguin Books Ltd, Bath Road, Harmondsworth, West Drayton, Middlesex UB7 0DA.*

In the United States: Please write to *Penguin Putnam Inc., P.O. Box 12289 Dept. B, Newark, New Jersey 07101-5289* or call 1-800-788-6262.

In Canada: Please write to *Penguin Books Canada Ltd, 10 Alcorn Avenue, Suite 300, Toronto, Ontario M4V 3B2.*

In Australia: Please write to *Penguin Books Australia Ltd, P.O. Box 257, Ringwood, Victoria 3134.*

In New Zealand: Please write to *Penguin Books (NZ) Ltd, Private Bag 102902, North Shore Mail Centre, Auckland 10.*

In India: Please write to *Penguin Books India Pvt Ltd, 11 Panchsheel Shopping Centre, Panchsheel Park, New Delhi 110 017.*

In the Netherlands: Please write to *Penguin Books Netherlands bv, Postbus 3507, NL-1001 AH Amsterdam.*

In Germany: Please write to *Penguin Books Deutschland GmbH, Metzlerstrasse 26, 60594 Frankfurt am Main.*

In Spain: Please write to *Penguin Books S. A., Bravo Murillo 19, 1° B, 28015 Madrid.*

In Italy: Please write to *Penguin Italia s.r.l., Via Benedetto Croce 2, 20094 Corsico, Milano.*

In France: Please write to *Penguin France, Le Carré Wilson, 62 rue Benjamin Baillaud, 31500 Toulouse.*

In Japan: Please write to *Penguin Books Japan Ltd, Kaneko Building, 2-3-25 Koraku, Bunkyo-Ku, Tokyo 112.*

In South Africa: Please write to *Penguin Books South Africa (Pty) Ltd, Private Bag X14, Parkview, 2122 Johannesburg.*